MARKETING
FOR THE SMALL
DESIGN FIRM

MARKETING FOR THE SMALL DESIGN FIRM

by Jim Morgan

WHITNEY LIBRARY OF DESIGN
an imprint of Watson-Guptill Publications/New York

TO MY DAUGHTERS SARAH, REBECCA, AND MARIA MORGAN
(especially to Becky and Maria who, by entering college simultaneously,
helped me to see the value of undertaking this project)

Copyright © 1984 by Jim Morgan

First published 1984 in New York by the Whitney Library of Design
an imprint of Watson-Guptill Publications,
a division of Billboard Publications, Inc.,
1515 Broadway, New York, N.Y. 10036

Library of Congress Cataloging in Publication Data
Morgan, Jim, 1934–
   Marketing for the small design firm.
   Bibliography: p.
Includes index.
   1. Design services—United States—Marketing.
I. Title.
NK1404.M58   1984   745.4′068   84-2239
ISBN 0-8230-7366-1

Distributed in the United Kingdom by Phaidon Press Ltd., Littlegate
House, St. Ebbe's St., Oxford

Manufactured in U.S.A.

First printing, 1984
2 3 4 5 6 7 8 9/89 88 87 86 85

Acknowledgments

MY THANKS AND GRATITUDE TO:

My sixteen respondent design firms for generously sharing their experiences and thoughts on marketing design services. Bill Koster, in particular, has earned my admiration. It was he who, in 1963, taught me most of what I knew about the business of architecture when I began my own practice. Koster has never stopped trying to learn about how better to serve his clients since then.

John Hagmann for reading the manuscript and offering suggestions for the visual organization of the book.

Carol McConochie for not only reading the manuscript but offering valuable help and information at several points during its preparation.

Judith Carrington for her advice at crucial moments as I worked on this book.

Dorothy Schaefer, my mother, who thirty years ago made possible my detour from architectural studies to Kenyon College where I learned to write.

Susan Davis for graceful, sympathetic copy editing.

Stephen Kliment for interest in the book that went far beyond the involvement required by his job as its editor. He constantly encouraged me to relate the manuscript to the needs of the reader, professional designers like ourselves. Thus concepts and ideas contained here were refined to a degree well beyond what they would have been without his benign guidance. The graphic exhibits that fill each chapter are especially the result of his desire to make the book useful to designers who have never yet made a "cold call" as well as to those more experienced marketers.

Finally, Barbara Ambrose, my wife and resident marketing expert, for her participation that began with our first discussions about how to organize the material, continued while I wrote it, and culminated in very thorough proofreading and commentary on the final manuscript. My deepest thanks for her loving support and patience.

Contents

Editor's Note

DESIGNERS WITH a modest-sized practice have for years complained about the lack of a guide that would show them how to go after new work without spending the large funds implied in existing books on marketing. At long last, Jim Morgan has written such a book. You don't, he says, for example, have to spend a fortune on brochures. What counts most, he points out, is to instill in your prospects a feeling of confidence in you as a designer and as a person.

How to do this and still make use of affordable printed and other promotional tools is the theme of this book. Morgan does it two ways: first, by means of text, sample pieces, and checklists and, second, by tracing the marketing experiences, both good and bad, of sixteen carefully chosen modest-size design firms—architects, interior designers, industrial designers, and graphic designers. These 16 profiles, arranged in groups of four throughout the book, are key to obtaining the most value out of this book. Based on the description of a creative marketing method, from initial search to successful selection by the client, this book offers the skills any modest-size design office can use to its great advantage.

Stephen A. Kliment
Executive Editor
Whitney Library of Design

*"When amateur
musicians
get together,
they talk
about music.
When professional
musicians gather,
they talk
about money."*

ANONYMOUS

Part One

FACING THE ISSUE

"M
ARKETING" IS A concept that many designers find offensive. We immediately think of advertising campaigns for things as different as toothpaste and housing developments and decide that marketing has no role in something as complex and individualized as design services. Unfortunately, when designers let such attitudes affect our business sense, we are making a big mistake.

Perhaps if two words, "promoting" and "selling," are substituted for marketing, the uncomfortable feelings you may have will begin to fade. After all, even designers recognize the need for self-promotion, especially through publication in certain magazines. "Selling," of course, is a word with bad connotations for some. But anyone who has made a vigorous effort to win a commission has to admit that "selling" is an integral part of practice. Promoting and selling are necessary if a design firm is going to do more than just survive from one year to the next. Profit, in our case, doesn't necessarily mean huge sums of money—just enough to reverse the crippling spiral of debt that is so easy for a design studio to fall into. A consistently pursued program of new business development offers you the stability to build a cohesive, experienced staff. It means your design skills can flourish and grow year by year, to say nothing of technical and project management abilities. Such a program also offers the possibility of having enough work so that you can be selective about the commissions you accept. It can help you create more effective promotional materials.

In short, marketing matters for designers.

Chapter One
MARKETING AS A DESIGN PROBLEM

NOT ONLY IS promoting and selling something that designers ought to do, but it is a part of professional life that can be as satisfying and fun as working out the solution to a visual problem. In the case of finding new clients, the media are not pen or pencil on paper but rather the give and take of human communication. Yes, there is a need for handsomely produced promotional materials. Yet the heart of what we are talking about here is reaching out to other people so that they will begin to trust you. The work you show them helps certify your skill, but what matters most of all is that they should feel you care about helping fulfill their needs.

Research, analysis, and synthesis is the three-step approach to solving design problems that was taught years ago in Carnegie Tech's architecture department. The idea was that you first study other people's work and ideas related to your problem. Then you analyze carefully what you have read and learned in order to identify the relevant information for solving the present problem. Finally you try various ways to combine and interpret that information until magically, through what was called the "intuitive leap," you would come upon the optimal answer based on the material you had to work with.

Marketing is also a three-part process that requires research and analysis before any meaningful synthesis is possible. Market research means investigating the businesses and areas where people are likely to welcome information about your office and its work. Analysis in this case means figuring out what strengths your firm offers, as well as what weaknesses. Both need to be dealt with in order to compete effectively with your peers for prospects' attention. It also means setting goals: determining what you want to gain from promoting and selling your services. Synthesis in marketing, and here persistence is the prime ingredient, is where you take what you have learned about the market and yourself and apply it to making contacts with potential clients. Just as design work is based on sketch after sketch, overlay on top of overlay, so marketing is the dogged effort of contacting one job prospect after another, learning from each one how to approach the next. And just as it is a thrill to see a design concept leap off the board where only seconds before there was nothing, so it is with winning a commission after working hard for it—especially when you outran the competition.

When you realize that promoting is talking about your own work and selling is learning about other people's needs and winning their trust, the effort will become less onerous, possibly even fun. And in the long

Definitions

Marketing: A step-by-step program to find and develop possible commissions based on self-chosen, long-term goals and self-analysis of your firm's capabilities. It consists of promoting and selling, both pursued as consistent, focused efforts at contacting prospects that are limited only by your firm's financial means and the time available.

Promotion: Vigorous outreach to sources of work identified through market research and referral. It is designed to pre-sell prospects with printed materials conveying an appropriate image of your firm and with telephone and personal contacts that emphasize your professional competence and your interest in solving that particular organization's set of design problems.

Selling: The process of convincing individuals that your firm is the one that will most thoroughly fulfill his or her needs and desires for a specific project. It requires listening to the client and restating his or her wishes in terms of your potential. Finally, it involves striking a balance between service and price that satisfies everyone.

run, promoting and selling establishes a secure economic framework for you. Within that you can then devote your energies more freely to what you like doing best.

WHAT DESIGNERS THINK ABOUT MARKETING

"THE WHOLE field has changed so much in the last fifteen years that it is really rather staggering," says interiors and furniture designer Gere Kavanaugh of Los Angeles. "Architectural interior design has grown faster than architecture. There is a refreshing attitude in the field these days. Designers just go out and get the business. The days when you could wait for people to come to you because you're so good—those days are past."

And that is what this book is about: going out and getting the business. It is about doing it on a small budget and that means doing it mostly yourself. Sixteen small American design firms share their thoughts on marketing here so that the point of view is both broader and more substantial than any one designer's experience. Kavanaugh and her colleagues were not chosen because they are experts at marketing. In fact, this group was selected to represent a cross-section of attitudes toward marketing, rather like those found among designers as a whole. Several of the offices, often quite small, some no more than studios, do not market in any organized way; on the other hand, one has a marketing director and two or three others, with a dozen or so professionals apiece, actively seek new clients. These offices range across the entire spectrum of design practice (excepting fashion and theater design). They are located throughout the United States, and with one or two exceptions they are not particularly well known to their peers.

What they share is a commitment to excellent design quality and a willingness to talk openly about their feelings toward promoting and selling their services. Each was asked to respond to a questionnaire (reproduced on page 27) that raises almost forty specific issues. Some of the participants wrote in remarkable detail. Others, interviewed verbally, responded in a conversational manner. That is why certain people are quoted at length, while others, who supplied short answers to the questions, are paraphrased.

GETTING OVER BAD FEELINGS ABOUT MARKETING

THIS IS MEANT to be a "user-friendly" book that takes into account the emotional barriers that can exist in a designer's mind when it comes to self-promotion. The author is not a marketing expert offering refined and esoteric advice. Rather, I am a designer who understands from experience the importance to successful practice of effective promotion and selling. Marketing principles and techniques are not difficult to understand. The question is whether or not a designer wants to apply them with vigor and consistency. This book can help you make that decision and then, if you choose, carry out an appropriate marketing program.

Let me introduce you to the material that follows by offering a personal case history of how *not* to market, which I learned the hard way. One motive for writing this book is to offer sound business advice to all the bright, ambitious designers who are just starting their own practices as I did in 1963 in Gambier, Ohio. May you benefit from what I have since learned.

I was one of those people who couldn't wait to start a practice after completing architecture studies, in this case, at MIT. Early in 1963, armed only with a license to practice, I hung up my shingle in Gambier, Ohio, the lovely village that is home to my alma mater, Kenyon College. With "superb" business sense and before a year had passed, I succeeded in alienating the trustees of the college, the only source of institutional work for several miles in any direction. At the same time, knowing nothing about real estate development, I decided to find backers for a faculty housing project in Gambier—10 three- and four-bedroom units that would rent for $100 a month to young professors with families. A brief account of what I learned from that about real estate development is on page 119 of the January 1973 *Architectural Record.*

Who knew anything about marketing design services in the early sixties? After six years of struggling to find enough work in that rural paradise, my practice and family life both collapsed under the never-absent financial pressures of a poorly conceived and operated business. I did in fact make an effort to promote myself: After a year or two of practice, a simple folder illustrating completed jobs and describing the intentions of the firm was printed and three hundred copies were mailed to savings and loan banks, lumberyards, and other businesses within fifty miles. Canvassing trips to colleges and other institutions in nearby towns were made. But I *never* followed up on any of these leads. It was stretching things to knock on doors at all; to call the prospects one had met afterwards or to write them a letter was considered impossibly pushy. Yet, in retrospect, follow-up might have made the difference between a marginal design practice and success. One other lesson I learned: You must strive for a modest profit from your firm; otherwise the price paid in mental anguish cancels out all the pleasure of being a designer.

Since those days, I have had the opportunity to see how many other designers do their work. I left for New York City and became a magazine writer and a teacher of both interior design and urban design while doing a bit of architecture from time to time. In those capacities I came to see that I was not the only designer who had trouble going out to make a sale. Thus this book is lovingly offered to any designer who cares to ponder the great mystery of finding new clients.

USING THIS BOOK

IF YOU HAVE already done some promoting and selling for your firm, you may wish to turn immediately to specific technical chapters. On the other hand, if marketing seems unfathomable to you, be sure to read the profiles of the sixteen design firms and how they deal with the issue. You will be relieved to see that some of them also have problems putting a program together. The profiles are intended to give you a sense of each firm's business personality. When you then read its response to a specific marketing question, you will better understand the reasons behind that office's approach.

Each of the book's five parts ends with a list of "Things to Do" and "Things to Avoid." Since these encapsulate the main items covered on the previous pages, you may find them a useful introduction to the section as well as a review. There is also an Appendix devoted to microcomputers and their role in the promotion and selling of design services. Finally there is a Selected Bibliography of books and other sources of information on marketing.

Identifying the Book's Principal Themes

Be persistent: Marketing is about reaching out to people.

Analyze your firm's strengths and weaknesses honestly.

Set realistic marketing goals based on your firm's financial means.

Design your program around your needs and interests.

Record your goals and marketing plan.

Identify your markets through careful research.

Involve as many of your staff in promotion of the office as possible.

Follow up on every letter, brochure, or portfolio that you send out.

Use interviews to ask questions, not to give a speech.

Good cost accounting helps you set fees in a convincing way.

Keep your promotional materials as flexible and inexpensive as possible.

Make sure you distribute your promotional materials widely.

Chapter Two
ANALYZING YOUR PRACTICE

Questions to Ask Yourself Before Setting Up a Marketing Program

How do your design goals affect your business goals?

What matters most to you as you go about your work?

What are your feelings about going after new clients?

Why are you running this business anyway?

WHY BOTHER to analyze your practice? All you want to do, after all, is get some more work—that's why you're reading this book, right? However, if the good news here is that there are many inexpensive ways to look for new clients, the bad news is that the way your practice works—how well it is organized—is directly related to how successful you will be at getting jobs.

The first logical step, therefore, to successful promotion is to truly understand what it is you have to sell. Let Bill Koster, a Cleveland architect with a small office, tell you why: "I first became concerned about marketing and economic stability when I read the AIA-sponsored Case Management Report in 1967. I was appalled at what my future business prospects appeared to be. Back in the late sixties there wasn't anything yet written about marketing for the design professions. I reacted to the demands of my clients for excellence in service, accuracy in budgeting, and careful follow-through on construction. Because of that I reached out to other professionals—that is, to business executives, accountants, lawyers, sales people, and teachers—seeking a better understanding of the reasons people build or try to improve their environment. I did not depend upon nor search out my fellow architects' advice or observations on business."

Koster proceeded to establish a small board of directors for his firm—business and marketing experts—who have helped him carry on a continuing analysis of the service his firm offers and the goals that it pursues. Such analysis need not be expensive. Nor need it be done by outsiders to be effective; any sort of honest look at your business will help you understand it better.

NINE FACTORS TO CONSIDER

THE NINE FACTORS that follow are intended to provide a framework for your self-study, not a gradeable test. After that are four other points that you may also wish to consider in the analysis of your firm.

DESIGN PHILOSOPHY. Although the design approach of a firm is not the only criterion for successful marketing, it is such an important issue to designers themselves that it seems wise to get it out of the way

How to Assess Your Own Finances

Do you use standard accounting methods to keep track of the firm's income and expenses?

How stable has the office been (size of staff, gross income, amount of work, and so on) over the past few years?

How much can you set aside for marketing each year?

Would setting aside 10 percent of last year's gross earnings for marketing (figure 80 percent of that amount for salaries and 20 percent for materials, overhead, and so forth) cause cash flow problems?

first. Very few other professional or commercial ventures have a "philosophy." Yet many designers have trouble separating their interest in visual matters from other aspects of their business.

Voorsanger and Mills, New York City architects who have in a few short years become identified with the best of Post-Modernism, do not have that problem. Based primarily on broad prior professional experience, Voorsanger and Mills have learned to let whichever of them is in charge of a project decide on the design values in that case. For business purposes they work together, relying on discussions with professional colleagues, their accountant, and their staff. "The most important way for us to evaluate our strengths and weaknesses," says Mills, "is through listening to outsiders' opinions (clients and prospective clients) and considering them objectively."

Gere Kavanaugh, whose diverse Los Angeles practice ranges across interior, graphic, and product design, has also seen her work widely published. Her business philosophy is based on "things I like to do." Like many other designers, she has gotten along quite well on referrals in the past. Now she has begun to set up a marketing program by asking herself questions like those in the accompanying box.

PRACTICE FINANCES. Every designer who opens an office soon realizes the effect of money on his or her ability to practice at all, let alone to do prize-winning work. Other sources of income can be important. Warren Infield and Frank D'Astolfo have eased into their New York City graphic design practice with the help of two teaching salaries—not as substantial as a trust fund might be, but enough to enable them to be selective about the work they accept. Most design offices experience alternating periods of not enough and then too much work. A basic reason for marketing design services is to stabilize the office's financial structure.

Joe Jordan and Jim Mitchell, two architects in Philadelphia, carried on an extensive dialog about finances and marketing before deciding to form a partnership in 1981. In addition to evaluating each other's design and technical skills, they established "a growth goal of twenty people within five years, a gross billings and profit plan, as well as a time allocation goal for marketing" during the negotiations.

SERVICE AND SERVICES. Have you ever stopped to figure out just what your firm actually offers clients? Like Pamela Waters, whose New York City practice covers environmental and graphic design (a very broad spectrum, in fact), many of us are ready to design anything that somebody will pay for. But design flexibility is only part of the story. Waters puts it this way: "Try to do good work and help your client constantly. That's how you get them to come back again: service." She sees it as an attitude that pervades every part of the process, sometimes referring potential clients to other, more appropriate designers. But even that has a benefit: Those clients often come back later "because they know I'm honest."

Another way to define that ambiguous term, "service," is as the various skills a firm can bring to a particular project. Will Ching, a New York City interior designer, incorporates these directly into his new business prospecting letters (see eight-point list in accompanying box).

Any design firm can state its offerings more clearly if it has thought through its strengths and potential for service. Marketing, in fact, requires such analysis because those seeking design service often have trouble keeping one firm straight from another—especially since more and more are using initials such as AKA or UDA as the firm name. Clearly defined professional services can help distinguish you from the competition.

Analyzing Your Service Capabilities

Have you become known for high-quality client service? Or are unhappy clients a constant, nagging problem?

What in the past have been the strongest services that you offer clients?

Is your firm strong in programming? In design/conceptual skills? In production capabilities? In technical development?

Do you have a "full-service" practice (feasibility studies, design and documentation, project management)?

Will Ching's List of Professional Services

Meeting the client's functional space and facilities requirements.

Designing with excellence and innovation.

Assigning staff with applicable experience.

Adhering to budgets and schedules.

Full and careful coordinating with the client's in-house staff.

Coordinating consultation services as required.

Working for highly competitive fees.

Establishing a personal commitment to each client.

SPECIALIZATION. The most logical way for a designer to approach promotion and selling is specialization (see section on specific markets on page 75). Whether you like that idea or not, it is useful to review the projects you have done in the past and look for threads of continuity and capitalize on them. For example, Alfredo De Vido is a New York architect well known for single-family house design. He happens also to have completed projects in three other areas: stores, offices, and theater renovations.

There is a strong potential in the field of theater renovations if the marketing experience of Jaffe Acoustics of Norwalk, Connecticut, is correct: "Because we are highly specialized as consultants and designers of theater acoustics, our competition is limited," explains Jaffe's marketing director, Ann Boyar. "Chris Jaffe's interest in the theater brought the company into this specialization. Our goal has been to get projects that have the prestige to help us receive recognition in the field. This, coupled with the firm's ability and innovativeness, enabled us to achieve a reputation as one of the major acousticians in the world for the performing arts." What a refreshingly clear self-assessment!

Your firm may shrink from proclaiming the world-class status of Jaffe's firm, but there is no reason why, after you have reviewed your strengths, you cannot state them just as clearly. Clients love the reassurance of an honest statement of your professional worth. After all that's the basis of most successful commercials.

PERSONNEL. From the marketing point of view, the staff of your design firm is probably its greatest untapped strength. Have you ever thought about asking everybody on your payroll to get involved in finding more projects? After all, they all stand to gain from a consistently full workload.

The experience of UDA Architects in Pittsburgh illustrates why such a policy reflects the attitude of treating your staff as professionals (including those involved in office and business management). "We find we have to retrain young architects who enter our firm," says David Lewis, the firm's senior partner, "since most architectural education is poor in urban design. We attempt to nurture and keep our young people for a long time. We therefore hire with permanence in mind." Why shouldn't these same young people participate in UDA's marketing program?

Look around your own drafting room and see whether there are individuals who could help you. At least, consider holding a "seminar" to acquaint everyone in the office with the importance of a formal process for seeking new clients.

When the firm is extremely small, as in the case of Radford-Biddison, interior designers in Reston, Virginia, all partners must be seriously involved in promotion and selling. "The beginning of our marketing plan was the identification of one principal (Radford) as responsible for the effort," say Pam Radford and Gail Biddison. "Although both principals market assiduously, one has the responsibility for keeping up with the publications which provide leads and information, for initial 'cold contacts' and follow-ups in general, for monitoring the whole marketing process."

PROJECT MANAGEMENT CAPABILITIES. From the client's standpoint, project management skills are at least as important as design reputation in the decision to commission a project from your firm rather than from somebody else. Budget/schedule control skills and project management experience in general are a key aspect of marketing success for every kind of designer. If you are not too good at it, now is as good a time as any to figure out why not. If you have a track record of efficiency, then make a lot out of it in your promotional materials.

Examining Your Specialization Potential

Do you avoid specialization?

Are you considered an expert in any area of design or practice?

What is your firm's history or project specialization (example by example)?

Could your office associate with others to offer a joint specialty with a variety of expertise [such as an architecture/engineering (A/E) joint venture in sophisticated medical facilities]?

Assessing Your Personnel Strengths

Do you have turnover problems, or is your staff stable, loyal, and enthusiastic?

Have you individuals on your staff who could carry out marketing support functions?

What are the individual qualities of your staff that could contribute to your marketing efforts?

What areas of expertise should be strengthened, or should personnel be brought in fresh to open new marketing possibilities?

Jordan/Mitchell is an architectural firm in Philadelphia that puts a strong emphasis on its efficiency in presentations, especially letting potential clients know that the firm uses its microcomputer as a means of meeting schedules and keeping track of project costs (for a discussion of the use of microcomputers in design work, see Appendix A). AKA Landscape Architects of Palo Alto, California, is another design firm that sells its services based on its record in budget control. Ken Arutunian, AKA's senior partner, finds that it is more difficult to meet completion schedules because of chronic underestimation of the time required.

PRACTICE LOCATION. There are two aspects to this particular factor of your business analysis: first, the physical nature of the building in which you work and its neighborhood; and, second, the undeveloped marketing possibilities in the immediate area. Ralph Appelbaum purposely placed his exhibition design firm in New York's Soho neighborhood because "the location bespeaks our concern with broad ideas, urban rebirth, the new culture in general, art and science in particular. I take visiting clients to the boutiques and the galleries so they'll think about the new and inexpensive exhibition techniques seen there."

Judith Chafee has done the same by setting up her Arizona architectural practice in four contiguous adobe houses in Tucson's historic district. She believes in encouraging concentration at her city's "traditional urban and geographic center through participation and renewal."

The second consideration is more germane to our subject than the physical nature of your studio. How thoroughly have you investigated the prospects of selling your services within ten or twelve miles of your own doorstep? It's something that everybody tends to ignore, and yet you can be more effective than with projects that require a lot of travel. Of course, there may be a prejudice against professional skill found next door simply because it is *too* close. As they say in Ohio: "An expert is any carpenter from more than twenty-five miles away."

LOCAL/REGIONAL ECONOMY. The original reasons why you established your office where you did probably had little to do with the potential of the regional economy. Or if you did consider that, how carefully did you study the growth possibilities of those businesses that are likely customers for your services?

Bill Koster built the marketing program of Koster and Holzheimer Architects around the municipal building and public library needs of Ohio towns within three hours' drive of their Cleveland office. Koster and Holzheimer keep very close track of every potential job in their specialties in sixty-two of the state's eighty-eight counties (as you can see from their map shown on page 93). The firm studies the economic indicators of their region's economy with the help of a professional marketing consultant there. For example, by such careful analysis, Koster discovered that an enormous potential existed for revamping turn-of-the-century Carnegie libraries within his marketing area. Even though the region has been experiencing very tough times, his firm has a dozen or more such projects on the boards at any given time.

On the other hand, when Gordon Perry opened his industrial design office in New York City, he could assume that with some hustling, he would find enough work in the metropolitan area to keep himself going. What he has since realized is that project opportunities come from all over the place. In 1983 he was traveling regularly to Wisconsin and Taiwan to service accounts. Thus his proximity to major airports has become more important than New York City's potential.

Cataloging Your Project Management Abilities

Have you documented the time table and cost of your past jobs?

Are there patterns of inaccuracy or irresponsibility that can be identified from your records?

If you have a strong record on budget and schedule control, do you emphasize it to prospective clients?

How can you improve your project management capabilities?

Reviewing Practice Location Considerations

Is your office cramped for space or unable to expand should a lot of new work come in?

Are there possibilities for work nearby that have never been tapped or even explored?

What are the likely kinds of work to be found within an hour's drive?

How do transportation networks and geography (hills, rivers, lakes) affect your practice?

NATIONAL ECONOMY. There are no nationwide patterns for designers, although architects have watched a steady overall decline in new construction for the past fifteen years. On the other hand, interior design and building renovation have experienced enormous growth over the same period. Thus the interior design profession has gotten much stronger, and architects have slowly realized that they must go after that market in order to survive.

In addition, the shift of national economic vigor to the southwest has meant that all kinds of designers there have had much more work than their peers elsewhere. Jeanne Hartnett, who runs a Chicago interior design firm of seven professionals, saw the Sunbelt possibilities several years ago and began a marketing program to establish her firm there.

Jaffe Associates is another firm that pursues a national market for acoustical consulting services. In their current market plan, they note that while few American communities are now planning new performing arts centers, there is a growing interest in preserving and reusing grand old movie houses for concert and drama programs. Thus the Jaffe firm is shifting its own focus.

Another consequence of a generally tighter national economy is that small, local design firms find that there is increasing competition from outside professionals. Not only are the big regional firms more interested in smaller jobs farther away from home than ever before, but national corporate-style design firms with elaborate promotional machinery are out "beating the bushes" for every possible lead.

USING YOUR BUSINESS EXPERIENCE

UNLIKE MOST PEOPLE who graduate from college and go to work, designers have the benefit of the apprenticeship tradition. That is critical because, depending on one's discipline and the design school he or she completes, the young designer has little or no business experience (although that lack is now being remedied by many schools). It means that the approach to business in general and marketing in particular of the apprentice's employer has an enormous effect on the young person. Therefore we may pick up not only good but bad marketing habits from our first bosses. Nonetheless those patterns tend to be the ones we follow later. For example, both Judith Chafee and the Voorsanger and Mills partnership had the experience of apprenticeship with distinguished, well-published architects (together a remarkable compendium of the big names of the sixties). That is where they all learned the value of publication in getting new clients. On the other hand, one reason why many of today's architects, as well as other designers, are self-conscious about going after clients now is what they apprenticed in times when there was more than enough work for everyone. But times have changed.

Another way to use prior experience is to base promotion of your own office (especially in the first few years after you establish it) in part at least on the work you did for previous employers. Naturally it is assumed that you give credit where such is due so that no misunderstandings develop as to your actual role in the projects shown in your portfolio. It is quite foolish to hide or obscure such facts. Any prospective client can be made to appreciate your contribution to the finished job if it was substantial. If it was not, then don't try to pass off your employer's work as your own. The fact is that your firm's qualification statement (as distinguished from a personal resume) can very properly list not only your previous employers but the names of clients whom you served while employed by them.

Facing the Realities of Your Local Regional Economy

Are things so slow that the size of your prospecting area should be substantially increased?

What are the business sectors in your area that will definitely *not* need your services?

What are the specific growth possibilities there that relate to your practice?

What is the long-term economic prospect for your region?

Looking for Opportunities in the National Economy

How does your firm deal with a deteriorating national economy?

How do foreseeable future trends in national consumer demand affect your design field in particular?

What potential economic developments can you capitalize upon?

How do population/age statistics influence future demand for your expertise?

MARKETING MULTIDISCIPLINARY DESIGN

SEVERAL OF THE design firms profiled in this book offer services that cross the traditional lines between fields. Gere Kavanaugh and Pamela Waters combine interior, graphic and product, or environmental design in lively, challenging practices. UDA Architects' work ranges from urban planning through architecture to preservation and reuse of historic buildings. Most of the architects also do interiors.

The concept of multidisciplinary design practice is an excellent idea. The problem is how to promote it to potential clients—firms and individuals—who specialize (and have trouble understanding designers who don't). If you have such a practice, you no doubt are seasoned at explaining to unbelievers how the design process can be applied to any problem requiring a physical solution. Yet no matter how informative, even entertaining, your speech may be, do you often feel that the prospect remains, deep down, unconvinced?

As you analyze your firm and begin to consider the marketing goals you wish to pursue, it is wise to isolate each traditional design discipline as you practice it from the others. Then analyze your firm, in turn, as though you do only one thing. For instance, if you do graphics, product design, and packaging, go through the list of nine factors shown on pages 15 – 19 and answer those questions (as well as any you wish to add) in terms of your attitude toward *graphics*. Then do the same for *product design,* followed by *packaging.* Make a three-column chart, and for each factor, state briefly your conclusions. This should help you set some priorities as to which field you will promote the hardest. But the decisions will be up to you—and all the more valuable because you will have deduced them yourself.

GETTING OUTSIDE HELP

NO ONE WILL THINK the worse of you if you decide you need some help doing this kind of self-analysis. Therefore, if you can afford it, you may want to find a consultant to help you make this study, if not assist with your entire marketing program. UDA Architects, for instance, have had three separate consultants, all of whom have helped the firm focus more clearly on its marketing intentions. They have worked with Diana Riddle of Riddle-Johnson, a graphic designer with marketing experience. She was valuable, in UDA's words, "for her ability to relate the design of marketing materials to her experience in marketing strategies." Another consultant was John Grant, a management consultant from the University of Pittsburgh. He helped UDA "articulate the firm's goals and therefore marketing goals," and he helped them confirm their commitment to urban design and planning. Finally, they retained David Barbour, a marketing consultant who calls himself a "propagandist." He urged UDA to focus its marketing on areas in which they are most interested and therefore perform best.

Koster and Holzheimer, as noted earlier, is a small architectural firm with a formal board of directors. The partners asked two Cleveland businessmen to permanently assist in running the practice. One is a Harvard MBA who runs a small chemical company and teaches at the local community college. He was asked to serve precisely because he offers no connections to design at all, just sound business advice. The other

---

Immediate Sources of Work and Promotion

Ask your former employers if there is any work that you could do as a subcontractor.

Approach contractors and suppliers (especially those with whom you have worked in the past) for leads and possible jobs.

If you have a specialty (or can define one based on prior work), contact individuals and organizations that might need such services.

Present yourself as a practicing professional to as many people in the following categories as you can: relatives, neighbors, church and PTA acquaintances, old school friends, local alumni of your school, everyone else you've ever met.

Join the Chamber of Commerce, the Rotary Club, and/or other service/social organizations.

Go see appropriate newspaper editors and arrange for articles announcing your new practice.

board member is a journalist who worked in the past as the business development manager for two large architectural firms. He has played a strong role in shaping Koster and Holzheimer's promotional communications.

STARTING FROM SCRATCH

IF YOU ARE JUST beginning to practice design, then promoting and selling your services may seem mysterious. If you've had the opportunity to work for a designer who is good at it, chances are you'll have some idea of how you want to go about it. If not, this book will explain why marketing is important and how to do it. Many designers open their practice as a result of being laid off by an employer. That's the hard way to do it for three reasons. First, most people's self-confidence is weakened by losing a job (even if they did nothing to cause it), and you need to feel especially sure of yourself to start a new business. Second, unless you've had a free-lance operation on the side, you are starting out with no clients or references. Third, you probably have very little capital to invest in the new venture.

Nonetheless you have a chance, with your clean slate, to go at practice in a rational way from the start. That includes setting goals and devising a marketing plan, no matter how modest. Most designers don't proceed in an organized fashion. As Gordon Perry, a New York packaging and product designer, says, "Goals? Most of mine have been forced on me by necessity. First—it was after I was laid off—to stay alive; and then it was to get enough to pay the rent and the bills; and now it is to keep my people and me in paychecks."

The main thing is to get out and let everyone know you are available. Send out an announcement of your new office, and then follow up every one with a telephone call. Above all, don't spend money on promotional materials yet. Put whatever you can afford into paying yourself to knock on doors and personally tell people you are ready to serve them.

Chapter Three
SETTING MARKETING GOALS

OF ALL THE ASPECTS of promoting and selling your services, the setting down of goals seems to be the most difficult for designers to understand. Let's begin by stating that design excellence is assumed throughout the book. Therefore "design quality" is not included here as a goal even though many of you believe—and properly indeed—that it has a strong influence on how a firm presents itself to prospective clients. No, marketing goals relate specifically to the business of design rather than to it as an art or science. Unless you have had unusual exposure to business prior to this, it should be no surprise that as a designer, you are unacquainted with marketing goals as a concept. But that doesn't mean you can bypass them if you wish to develop a successful promotion and sales program for your firm.

SIX GOALS IN MARKETING DESIGN

THE SIX GOALS that follow are defined and formulated to capture the essence of design practice rather than business in general. You may find, based on other sources of information, that there are other goals that should be included or that some of these need adjusting to meet your needs. By all means, add and/or adjust at will! Rank them or not as you wish. Just don't ignore this step.

DIVERSITY. Whether as a designer you "specialize" or not, you will surely seek varied design experiences as you proceed through your career. So even if you do nothing but hospital design or book jackets, you still welcome the challenge of a new problem. That means that your marketing program (especially if you run a small office) must be conceived as a celebration of your broad interests and skills. It is likely that the more boldly you express and promote the range of your strengths the better. The goal, then, is to design a program that emphasizes to the prospect the advantages of your "fresh approach." At the same time, base your presentation on examples of proven experience and skill in making money for your clients. Whether diversity is your prime goal or not, decide what it means to you as clearly as possible and then set out to sell it.

CLIENT SELECTIVITY. Perhaps the ultimate goal of every designer is to choose only those clients whom he or she wishes to serve. That desire stems not only from budgetary considerations but also from the technical and functional challenges of the project. It also implies the right chemistry with those commissioning the work. Naturally, such criteria are hard to fulfill. But you can raise the quality of jobs offered to your firm through a well-focused program of promotion and selling. The way to achieve this goal is: first to have at all times enough work in process so that you can afford to say "no" to any job you don't want; second to have well-developed selling techniques that enable you to go after and win the commissions you do want.

Radford-Biddison does it this way: "It has become clear that we are not suited to every job nor to all clients. Large jobs or those where very little "design" is wanted are not appropriate. They create a philosophical gap that is ultimately frustrating to our client and to us. Originally, we contacted everyone about everything we read or heard. It was not at all productive. Our goals now are more specific. We evaluate projects based on how they match our philosophy and basic strengths including personal compatibility with the client. We also look for a profit."

STABILITY. In marketing for normal businesses, this goal would be called "growth." Not so for designers, based on the comments of the sixteen firms participating here and many other informed sources. The standard concept of 4-to-10 percent annual increase in size and sales as an index of the health of a design practice is irrelevant. Instead the emphasis for marketing success is on avoiding the hire-and-fire syndrome that so often weakens—indeed destroys—the morale of design practices. The goal therefore is to design a promotion and sales program that will level off the extremes of too much/not enough work so that you can build a truly professional staff. That means being able to offer at least a few excellent people the kind of security that is taken for granted in most other businesses.

The idea of stability does not preclude actual growth in the firm, of course. By developing three-year projections of cash flow, income, and numbers of projects (as Koster and Holzheimer have) you can insure opportunities to hire gifted associates as permanent colleagues. Jordan/ Mitchell is an example of a firm dedicated to this kind of controlled growth. In J/M's words, "Organized marketing stands high on the list of ingredients we feel have contributed to our increase from four people initially to the current staff of ten."

LARGER MARKET SHARE. If you do specialize in one or more markets, then an extremely important goal is to get more of whatever work of that sort is available in your marketing area. This is where research and planning assume a central role. As you may imagine, achieving such a goal takes time. The key is to increase your share gradually, but consistently, within a given market. By building interest in your firm through patient tracking down of leads and persistent contact, you slowly become known among the individuals who are the decision makers of that circle.

Jeanne Hartnett's firm follows a vigorous pattern of contact and follow-up with potential clients in each of their four specialties. Yet, as she says, "It takes at least six months, usually one year, before this action begins to pay off. This is very important to know [underlining by JH]. Just because one has worked on a brochure and it looks impressive, one tends to believe it will be perceived by all who receive it as the answer to their problems. This is most often not the case, and while they are initially impressed, there are many factors that enter into a final choice. The best one can hope to do is get their attention. Then you have to get them to really focus on your firm. That takes work."

HIGHER FEES. In the advertising business, particularly, the annual billings of a firm are cited to describe both its relative size and its suc-

Goal Statement

Stability: Make up through marketing the difference between estimated income and targeted annual budget (not including projected profits).

Larger share of market: Seek to raise percentage of fees your firm gets from those estimated to be available from specific prospects in the geographic marketing area.

Diversity: Identify one or more new markets and sources of work in them; aim for a stated percentage of total income from them.

Adequate return: Develop marketing efforts that will increase total annual income to include a stated percentage for profit.

Client selectivity: Increase marketing efforts so that (1) there is enough work in the office to allow a stated percentage of expected referral work to be refused; and (2) approach a stated number of identified premium prospects and make every effort to win commissions.

Higher fees: Through publicity and other promotion efforts, raise the public image of your firm to justify asking for higher fees.

cess. In the design field, the total amount of fees billed each year is less useful an indicator of financial vigor than the amount of income generated per professional staff member. That figure serves to illustrate, among other things, the relative size of fees received by different offices for essentially the same amount of work (assuming that all design firms are equally efficient). As Infield + D'Astolfo realized soon after beginning their practice, it is far better to have fewer jobs with bigger fees from each than to run yourself ragged doing many low-budget, low-fee projects. If your records show that income per professional employee is inadequate, marketing can help increase your credibility, thus allowing you to ask higher fees.

Vigorous promotion helps you appear more substantial to clients who would otherwise deal with larger design firms. Gordon Perry makes the connection: "As part of trying to establish a firm financial base, I now approach larger companies. That's possible because I have developed stronger credentials in the last couple of years. That's the way to go since larger companies can pay larger fees and sustain larger projects. By the way, these projects usually wind up being a lot more interesting and educational than smaller jobs."

ADEQUATE RETURN. Ralph Appelbaum suggests that the issue of adequate return is to operate the office carefully enough so that you always know where the line between profit and loss lies—and then be sure you come down on the plus side. If you know exactly how much money you must get out of a job to meet that standard, chances are that you will convince the client that your fee is appropriate.

None of this is to say that a design firm shouldn't strive for a normal profit. It is always an important business goal. No firm can keep practicing design at a loss without serious psychological and financial consequences. Designers with outside income, no matter what the source, can afford to run a not-for-profit studio. The rest court disaster.

PROFITING FROM YOUR GOALS

ONCE GOALS ARE defined, they must be quantified. In a marketing program, goals are represented by specific quotas by which promoting and selling efforts can be measured later. If your main goal is a *larger share of the markets* you specialize in, then the quota is a percentage: Out of $250 million in hospital design contracts to be awarded next year in your marketing area, let's say, you strive to increase your firm's share from 6 percent to 9 percent of the total. *Stability* means setting an income level for next year that will more than meet your anticipated expenses; then you decide how much selling will be needed to bring in that amount in fees. *Adequate return* is the amount beyond that necessary for stability. It translates into money for investment in securities, retirement accounts, or real estate. Many design firms now have profit-sharing programs. Instead of relying on fate to determine how much there will be to divide up next Christmas, they set as a target a definite percentage of gross annual income (15 to 20 percent is realistic). *Higher fees* can be accurately determined by comparing last year's receipts with the number of hours actually billed. *Client selectivity* requires that you identify a certain number of prospects—firms or individuals—for whom you would like to work and then go after each of them, with the intention of winning a job within a year or some other specified time period. *Diversity* is a more difficult goal to quantify. It means picking a new commercial or institutional field or variant that you want to work in and then gearing up to go after

What Higher Design Fees Can Mean

Corporate Design magazine, in its annual list of the "100 Biggest Interior Design Firms," confers position based on total annual dollar volume of a firm's projects. It also lists total fees, total square footage, and total volume per employee. Between the top two firms in 1981–1982, total volume was very close: $212 million versus $200 million, a spread of only 5 percent and significantly ahead of firm number three. Volume per employee for these two giants was quite a different story: $5,171,000 for number one versus $568,000 for its rival, almost nine times larger! That is because the first office has 41 professionals and the second has 352. Without considering the differences in overhead between the two, the figures show that annual income of the first firm is $12,000 per person higher than that of the runner-up.

jobs there. First you must master the needs of that market or field and determine the sources of available work. Then you must figure out how to go after those jobs.

Pamela Waters provides a good example of that process: After she went to the New York Boat Show a year or two ago, she decided it would be fun to have pictures of motor cruisers and sailboats around the office. So she began actively to seek graphics work from manufacturers in that business. She realizes that she must spend at least a year and aim at getting four or five worthwhile jobs if her diversification strategy is to succeed.

If you work consistently toward the marketing goals you set for yourself, says Ann Boyar of Jaffe Acoustics, then there is no doubt your business will prosper. Her firm has worked hard to establish a reputation, and the staff has gotten considerably larger (up to seven professionals) as a result. Jaffe has increased its market share, and now attention is focused on building fees and cash flow. Profit accrues to such a business as a result of maintaining its clearly defined goals.

MODIFYING YOUR GOALS

IF THE GOALS described above do not fit your needs, revise them to apply to you and your field. Consider the differences between graphic design practice and architecture, for instance. Diversity in graphic design is likely to be much more important than stability, while the opposite is true in architecture where many firms specialize. Along with diversity, the graphic designer may be also seeking recognition. There are many more competitions and awards programs in graphics than in other design fields. Thus effort put into winning prizes could well be a marketing goal for those designers. On the other hand, a firm like UDA Architects has as one of its aims the nurturing of the urban design field itself through public awareness work by its principals. Since that also helps create opportunities for the firm, such a strategy is an important marketing goal for them.

Where you practice can have a substantial influence on your choice of goals. A small town or rural design firm is subject to certain conventions of business etiquette. The intense promotional efforts needed to obtain a larger market share, for instance, in the urban business world might seem so inappropriate as to be counterproductive. Choose your goals to fit your needs; then shape your marketing plan around them.

LETTING YOUR GOALS EVOLVE

IN ADDITION to the differences between design disciplines that can modify goals, there is the effect of time upon your plans. If you have never before pursued a formal program of promotion and sales, then the first six months of reaching out will teach you a great deal indeed. Ideas that now seem clear and logical may prove fruitless, but along the way you will determine new directions that will later lead to results.

For instance, you may start marketing by pursuing diversity for your graphic design practice only to discover that a brochure you did for a local bank has been unexpectedly effective. It can lead to more work from other financial institutions if you focus on selling to them; thus a year later, a larger share of this specific market becomes your primary goal. It means that not only your promoting and selling sharpen but your basic goals will change too. There's nothing wrong with that, especially if you have written them down along the way and can keep track of how your marketing attitudes have matured.

Every designer who has attempted serious promoting and selling accepts its experimental character. "The development of our 'plan' was evolutionary in nature," says Gail Biddison, "and did not begin with a structured format. A considerable portion of our first several months of operation was devoted to identifying goals. Then they evolved as we came to understand the firm's strengths and weaknesses. The cost of our time was probably much too high, based as our process was on trial and error. But otherwise we spent very little money on it."

Things to Do	*Things to Avoid*
Be honest with yourself and your colleagues during the assessment process.	**Trying to market** without first clarifying and examining your firm's goals.
Examine your motives for not wanting to specialize, and if you decide to emphasize diversity, promote and sell it with vigor.	**Keeping your** marketing goals in your head rather than writing them down.
Find advisors to help you develop your selling techniques and organize your market research.	**Beginning a promotion** and sales program before you assess your firm's abilities and limitations.
Take courses in marketing and selling at a local university or community college.	**Promoting in** an unfocused way—that is, not identifying the markets, or at least general areas, at which you aim.
Keep your cash-flow limitations in mind when setting goals for your marketing program.	**Letting your** "design convictions" get confused with your business objectives.
Examine your project management patterns in order to strengthen your firm's value to clients for meeting budgets and deadlines.	**Seeking commissions** that are too big for your present staff so that you will have to hire a lot of people and then fire them.
Quantify your goals in terms of specific annual quotas.	**Spending a lot** of money on promotional materials if you are just beginning practice.
Let your goals evolve as your marketing experience grows.	**Thinking that** "good designers" don't have to market.

Here is the questionnaire that was sent to the sixteen participating design firms to solicit their profiles.

A. How Did You Determine Your Marketing Goals?
How did you rank your criteria: Growth, Billings, Specialization, Profitability, etc.?
What process did you follow to define your goals?
How much time and/or money did you spend figuring out your goals?
How did your goals evolve after you began to market with a plan?
What shortcuts or pitfalls would you share with readers?

B. How Did You Assess Your Firm's Strengths and Weaknesses?
How did you study these factors: personnel, services, building types experience, budget/schedule
    control skills, project management capabilities, practice finances, practice location, practice
    philosophy or design values?
How have you compared your services to those of competing professionals?
Did you have outside help for this analysis? From whom?
How have you specialized as a result of setting your marketing goals?
What shortcuts or pitfalls came out of the assessment process for you?

C. How Did You Develop Your Marketing Plan?
What role did the following play: reference books, consultants or staff person for marketing,
    seminars, prior business experience, a "mentor" good at marketing, etc.?
What percentage of your gross annual billings did you allot for marketing?
Into what categories or proportions did you allocate those funds?
What is the time-span of your plan? How often do you revise it?
How much time per week per principal is spent on marketing?
How much did creating this plan cost you in time and/or money?
Did you develop work forms, charts, schedules, checklists, etc., that you wish to share with the
    readers?
What shortcuts or pitfalls occurred at this stage for you?

D. How Do You Find and Follow Up on Your Contacts?
Which of your sources for information on potential commissions yield the most results?
How do you make your first contact with potential clients?
How do you prepare for a specific interview?
How do you handle interviews in which other firms are competing?
What do you do after the interview as follow-up?
How do you negotiate the fee and close the deal?
Any special suggestions or warnings regarding this part of the process?

E. How Do You Use Promotional Materials?
How do you present your firm's work and design potential?
How do you make use of visual media (portfolios, slides, video, film, etc.)?
How can promotional materials be done on a small budget and still be attractive?
What is your sequence of mailings sent to potential clients?
What ideas/concepts/techniques work best to win you jobs?
What role does professional photography play in your presentations?

Please Respond in Terms Specific to Your Design Discipline or Fields of Interest.

AKA, Inc.

124 University Avenue,
Suite 202, Palo Alto, California 94301

Landscape Architecture

Established: 1968

Staff (mid-1983): Principal, two designers, secretary

Educational Background:
Kenneth A. Arutunian, ASLA:
B.A. (Landscape Arch.),
California Polytechnic Institute
(Pomona);
M.L.A., Harvard University

Professional Society:
American Society of Landscape
Architects (ASLA)

Kenneth Arutunian

PROFESSIONAL FRAMEWORK. In the sixteen years since he began his practice, Kenneth Arutunian has run the office three different ways. First, as an individual practitioner, he worked from his home. Then, when his staff grew to four or five people, he moved into an office in downtown Palo Alto, home of Stanford University. Later, in the mid-seventies, he formed a partnership and employed as many as ten people. Currently, he operates a sole proprietorship with a staff of three.

Having seen his firm grow quite rapidly during his partnership days, he has decided the present size is better for him. "We feel there are certain headaches associated with a larger staff (keeping enough work in the office, individual growth, personnel changes because people move on, etc.). A small, loyal cadre of good qualified professionals is our goal. My staff consists of two designers (landscape architects)—one of whom has been with AKA for seven years and the other for three years—in addition to a secretary and myself."

GOALS AND OBJECTIVES. Growth as such has not been a goal of the practice from its inception, says Arutunian. Instead he is seeking to broaden the types of projects the office works on so that he and his staff can enjoy greater variety in work assignments. "We have taken the position that diversity is economically more viable for the firm than specialization. We did landscaping for multiple housing in the early years, then more public agency work—parks and recreational facilities—until Proposition Thirteen [California tax initiative] took care of that in the late seventies. So we've watched two sources of specialized work dry up that had previously seemed endless." Increased fees is AKA's other business goal. Arutunian finds that he needs 20 percent more income over business expenses in order to compensate the staff well and make a profit. In recent years, the firm has been breaking even.

MARKETING STRATEGY. Over the past few years, almost all of AKA's promotion efforts have been focused

Four-page brochure on brown-tinted paper depicts projects and lists clients.

on getting specific jobs rather than canvassing for new business among prospects whom the firm has had no dealings with before. That is, of course, a consequence of the fact that landscape architects normally work as subcontractors or consultants to an architect or architecture/engineering (A/E) firm that holds the prime contract for the job (for further discussion see page 77). Most of AKA's efforts, therefore, have gone into selling rather than promotion. Accepting the fact that his firm is small, Arutunian has tried to screen the jobs that the firm goes after so that they only pursue projects appropriate to their size and those they have a realistic chance of obtaining. For a specialist design firm, that is an important general principle.

PROMOTION TACTICS. This firm of landscape architects has gotten along for many years on referrals from architects and other designers who held the prime contract for big jobs. When they have been asked to make a joint proposal, AKA has prepared its presentation inexpensively, usu-

ally mounting copies of drawings and photographs of relevant jobs on illustration board rather than making these into slides. It is a way, they have found, of using staff time effectively rather than outside sources.

PROMOTION MATERIALS. In the light of the firm's decision to go after diversified work within its specialty, AKA recently created a brochure for direct mail and other promotional use that emphasizes the breadth of their completed work. In keeping with the office's practice of producing all promotional and presentation pieces in house, this four-page self-mailer is on heavy stock similar to their standard tan letterhead. A series of small, informal photographs on three of the pages shows a wide range of completed jobs. All the copy and the larger type emphasize the variety of work, rather than landscape architecture as a discipline. It is a low-budget piece (less than $1 per copy to print), yet if AKA follows up vigorously on the 500 copies that were mailed out, it could be an effective way to bring in more work.

EVALUATION. Although AKA has never had a formal marketing plan, as the firm has matured, the goals of diversity and higher fees have come forward. These are crucial to the firm's health as a professional organization. AKA is not wasting money on glossy fliers and brochures; nonetheless its substantial body of clients and completed projects will help them win jobs if Arutunian and his associates set up active contact with the people to whom they have sent the mailer. Follow-up makes the difference between a significant number of new jobs and the 1 or 2 percent return that can be expected from a direct mailing with no further action.

AKA's work ranges from the geometric to the bucolic as the firm serves a broad spectrum of public, institutional, and commercial clients. Shown here are the Santa Clara County Civic Center (left) and Veterans Administration Hospital in Loma Linda, California (above).

Ralph Appelbaum Associates Incorporated

109 Greene Street,
New York City 10012
Museum planning and exhibition
design with a specialty in information
and visitor centers

Established: 1978

Staff:
Principal, industrial, interior
and graphic designers, architects,
technologists, writers, administration
(twelve people total)

Educational Background:
B.I.D., Pratt Institute

Teaching Position:
Adjunct Assistant Professor,
Museum Studies Program,
Graduate School of Arts and Sciences,
New York University

Professional Society:
Industrial Design Society of America
(IDSA)

Photo: © Elaine Guttman

Ralph Appelbaum

PROFESSIONAL FRAMEWORK.
Ralph Appelbaum's practice has
emerged in the eighties from a long,
informal "childhood"—as he puts
it—into an organized, compartmentalized format. For many years he
was primarily a consultant and
teacher, but as time passed, he has
found a strong and specific market
for his services in two areas. The
first, with which he long has been
associated, is exhibition design for
natural history and science
museums. Later he developed
another application for his firm's
skills: interpreting to the layperson
high-technology concepts and proc-
esses for corporations in the health,
energy, and computer fields. For
instance, visitors to a coal gasifica-
tion plant may never see the actual
buildings where the process takes
place. Instead they are taken through
a computer-controlled information
center where interactive exhibits and
media are shown to them, exhibits
designed by a firm like Appelbaum's.
In many cases it is the first time anyone has tried to explain these ideas
in popular terms. Thus Appelbaum
maintains an interdisciplinary staff of
professionals who have a specific
interest in the firm's work. Up to
now the practice has grown through
referrals and with the strong support
of past museum clients. It was only
as his firm expanded to a dozen
employees that Appelbaum began to
think about marketing.

GOALS AND OBJECTIVES. The twin
goals, in Appelbaum's words, are
"Diversity within a specialty, selectivity among clients." In his words,
"Marketing is deciding what jobs you
want." He looks for clients who find
appealing a multifarious practice
such as his, who are attracted to it by
what he calls, "personality comple-
ments." Clarifying the personality or
character of his firm so that potential
clients perceive its uniqueness is one
of Appelbaum's objectives in analyzing his practice. He believes it will
strengthen subsequent marketing
efforts. The office grew out of a studio, which, in the beginning,
absorbed all his energy. It has taken
years, he says, to be able to examine
it objectively and establish business
goals.

Stability is another attraction that
organized promoting and sales holds
for Appelbaum as his firm rapidly
expands. Not only does he see the
value of marketing in minimizing
the effect of slow periods, but "by
cutting the highs as well, you don't
have too many people when excessive
work dries up."

MARKETING STRATEGY. Up to
now, Appelbaum has been able to
grow by "letting the work speak for
itself." Publication in magazines that
museum curators read has been the
best form of publicity. He has perceived himself as a "non-marketer,"
an ambivalent attitude toward pro-

The broad range of Appelbaum's design
approach is illustrated by this show at
New York City's Museum of Natural
History. His firm did the banner as well
as the exhibits describing how
archeologists uncovered one of Mexico's
major Aztec temples.

motion and selling that is not uncommon among younger designers whose offices continue to have interesting and plentiful project opportunities. He prefers to see his business as an "art-oriented educational services group"—serving the public interest through interpretive exhibits in science museums. Thus he has promoted the enterprise primarily through speeches to responsive audiences at museum conventions and professional meetings and in recent years by teaching at New York University's postgraduate program for curators. This kind of visibility helps Appelbaum be seen as a designer interested in raising the quality of museums as a whole. He believes that it also puts the socializing related to marketing in a more dignified context.

PROMOTION TACTICS. In the museum world, although the client is the museum's manager and the board of trustees, the curator in charge of a project actually selects its designer. Thus it is the younger, more idealistic staff members who make recommendations to the older, experienced business people. In this case, Appelbaum's emphasis on design philosophy—coupled with a serious interest in the knowledge and passions of the museum scholar—has resulted in commissions. Acting as a catalyst, he says, he then brings the curators to his Soho studio and there helps them develop the exhibition's program.

EVALUATION. Appelbaum recognizes that "designers often feel guilty that they're not artists and that they must charge for their services." He wants to avoid marketing that is too obvious or high pressure. "Designers fear marketing, indeed they feel tainted by it," he says. "They may want the fruits of self-promotion, but they hate the stigma attached to selling." Nonetheless, as he prepares to seek corporate work, he is making adjustments that will help representatives of those organizations be comfortable with his design approach.

Judith Chafee Architect

317 North Court Avenue,
Tucson, Arizona 85701

Residential Architecture

Established: 1970

Staff (1983): Principal, three drafters, administrative assistant

Educational Background:
B.A., Bennington College;
B. Arch., M. Arch., Yale University

Teaching Position:
Adjunct Professor of Architecture, University of Arizona

Professional Societies:
Fellow, American Institute of Architects (AIA);
Fellow, American Academy in Rome

Judith Chafee

PROFESSIONAL FRAMEWORK.
Judith Chafee surprised many people in Tucson when she returned there from Connecticut in 1970 to set up her practice. She moved into four small, contiguous but dilapidated adobe houses in the Presidio, the original downtown of that sprawling city, and turned them into living/working space. She brought certain design standards with her from New Haven where she studied and worked for more than a dozen years. Chafee seeks to capture in her residential architecture the essence of Arizona's forbidding but beautiful terrain. As a design critic at the University of Arizona's College of Architecture, she finds clients among professionals who have moved to Arizona from the east. Her "regionalism" appeals to their sense of living in the desert, not in an air-conditioned box that might also be built in Chicago or Atlanta.

GOALS AND OBJECTIVES. Chafee left Connecticut because she wanted to practice independently; with neither the financial means nor the social connections to establish an office there, she says, "I decided to get the hell out. I had grown up in Tucson and although I had been away twenty years, it was the only other place I was really connected to. I made a scouting trip: talked to local architects, real estate people, the school of architecture at the University and acquainted myself with the new scale and character of the city. I decided it would be possible to establish a dignified office on a shoestring here. I also decided that I had sufficient design maturity to operate in a very lonely design situation. There is very little architecture, or interest in it, in Tucson. It took about ten years to reach a point where I felt the office was really established."

MARKETING STRATEGY. Because of her early training with Paul Rudolph, The Architects Collaborative, Kevin Roche, and Edward Larrabee Barnes, Chafee felt that "publication was my only hope to create a respected professional image. First I had to put in the design time to make the work worth publishing. Second it had to be seen by people who could help to get it published. That takes time too. Many small design firms in this region that start out to get commercial work through aggressive marketing view architectural publication as an elitist pastime. On the contrary, it has been my bread and butter. A very small firm, particularly (alas) with a woman principal, has got to have some authoritative approbation to gain credence. As it stands, publication and my teaching position provide the major sources of security for prospective clients."

PROMOTION TACTICS. The primary technique, then, that Judith Chafee has used to build her reputa-

tion is design quality. But that, in Arizona, as she points out, or in most other parts of the United States is not a sure-fire way to attract clients. So she developed another marketing idea that has been helpful in winning jobs. Studies were made of ways to use independent experts so that they seem to be part of Chafee's "regular service team," available only through her office. Depending on the project that the firm was after, the "team" has included structural, mechanical, and electrical engineers, an accountant, lawyer, landscape architect, native growth specialist, graphic designer, and/or a cost consultant. This approach has helped Chafee sell the idea that small commercial building projects, educational facilities, and multi-family housing jobs can benefit from this combination of professional expertise and her ability to give them a personal and unique design image. By 1983, the marketing effort was bringing in nonresidential commissions.

PROMOTION MATERIALS. In addition to nearly a dozen articles published in New York-based architecture and consumer magazines, Chafee has seen her work appear frequently in western and Japanese publications, particularly in *Sunset Magazine* (thirteen articles). Full-page feature stories on the front page of the *Arizona Daily Star's* and *Los Angeles Times'* Sunday Home sections, which include four-color photography, have also been useful to her. Professional-quality photography, in her opinion, has been the single most valuable tool in marketing the firm's design services.

EVALUATION. Chafee points out that promoting and selling her design services has brought her an unforeseen benefit beyond designing houses and seeing them built. In most cases it has meant that the owners have become friends and boosters of the practice. She invites them, their families, her contractors, and some of the craftsmen who work on the houses to a big Christmas party.

Quality of photography is a key selling medium for Judith Chafee, who has developed a reputation for houses that relate well to the Arizona desert, both shown here are in Tucson, while offering comfortable, energy-efficient living accommodations. The Jacobson residence is shown below; the Johnson house, above.

Photos: Glen Allison

Will Ching Planning and Design

81 Wooster Street,
New York 10012

Contract interior design

Established: 1978

Educational Background:
B.F.A. (interior design), Pratt Institute

Teaching Position:
Visiting Instructor of Interior Design,
Pratt Institute

Professional Societies:
American Society of Interior Designers
(ASID);
Vice President of Membership,
New York Chapter, Institute of Business
Designers (IBD);
Council member, National Council for
Interior Design Qualification (NCIDQ)

Photo: John Stern

Will Ching

(Right) Folder contains photographs,
partial listing of clients, drawings, and
listing of services. This insert illustrates
four of Ching's services; the back
contains written descriptions of each.

(Opposite page above) Will Ching
markets his firm as an interior design
organization that satisfies functional
and budget requirements without
sacrificing the style and comfort that
corporate executives have come to
expect as their perquisite, as shown
here in this office for Westco Insurance
Co. Inc.

(Opposite page below) Promotional
letter from Ching is couched in terms of
the client's key concerns, especially his
need for a smooth-running business.
The letter is limited to one page and
refers the reader to attachments (such as
the one shown here) that carry greater
detail about Ching's firm.

PROFESSIONAL FRAMEWORK.
Will Ching operates his office from a
sunny Soho loft as an individual
practitioner. The space is designed to
expand to five or six work stations as
business develops. Interior architecture (creating total interior envi-
ronments that integrate architectural
elements with user functions) is how
Ching describes his approach. It is
based on a strong background in
space planning and furniture specification but includes graphics,
planting, and art programs as well.
He is in charge of membership for
the New York Chapter of IBD and
concerns himself with professional
education and development as well.
Thus, as one of IBD's representatives,
he monitors and upgrades the

NCIDQ examination created by the
profession to establish standards for
interior designers.

GOALS AND OBJECTIVES. Having
begun his business with a referral,
Ching had two busy years. Then he
experienced an unexpected slowdown
when the calls stopped coming in.
That forced him to begin a marketing program whose principal goal is
stability. Ching is not interested in
growth as such because he feels that
a staff of five or six people is the
maximum size he could keep track of
and still do most of the design.
Because of his strong background in
space planning and office interiors,
Ching specializes in that field. Thus
another goal of his program is to

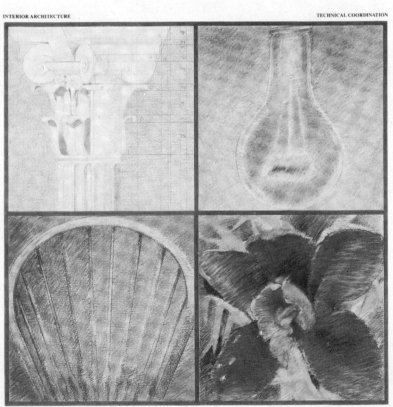

INTERIOR ARCHITECTURE

TECHNICAL COORDINATION

FURNITURE & FURNISHINGS PROGRAMS

PLANTING & ART PROGRAMS

WILL
CHING
PLANNING
& DESIGN

increase his firm's share in what is a vigorous New York market.

MARKETING STRATEGY. In 1981, Ching hired, as a short-term consultant, the marketing manager of a large New York City interior design and architecture office. This expert proposed a twelve-point program that included specialization suggestions, strategies for reaching those markets, a range of tools and monitoring procedures, as well as a job description for the marketing-support person whom Ching subsequently hired to carry out the program. All this was supplied for a fee of about $50 an hour.

PROMOTION TACTICS. Sunsh Stein had no marketing background when Ching hired her for part-time promo-

tion and administrative work in March 1982. She had worked in the advertising and editorial fields, however, and she was effective with the telephone. Stein brings a low-key, methodical approach to the firm's marketing program that guarantees consistent follow-up. They began by mailing a cover letter (see checklist on page 16) and folder of printed materials to a list of Fortune 500 companies in the New York City region. Stein often calls beforehand to get the name and title of the appropriate individual at the company. Subsequently, they also acquired lists of banks, of lawyers, and of local architectural firms to whom they wrote. Stein tries to make twenty follow-up calls each week, but since she also does billing

---

C
WILL
CHING
PLANNING
& DESIGN

PARTIAL LIST OF REPRESENTATIVE CLIENTS

Client/Location	Project Design
Penske Corporate Headquarters Piscataway, NJ	4,500 square feet Space Planning Interior Design Art Program
Morgens, Waterfall & Co. Inc. Rockefeller Center, NYC	2,000 square feet Space Planning Interior Design
Purolator Products Co. Rahway, NJ	8,000 square feet Refurbishing Furniture & Furnishings Art Program
Channing Weinberg New York, NY	17,800 square feet Space Planning Interior Design
Alcoa Corporation New Canaan, CT	13,000 square feet Space Planning Interior Design
The Small & Medium Industry Bank - Korea Seagram's Bldg., NYC	2,000 square feet Space Planning Interior Design
Westco Insurance Group Ramsey, NJ	20,000 square feet Program Development Lease Negotiation Space Planning Interior Design Art Program
Hertz Penske Truck Leasing, Inc. Parsippany, NJ	41,000 square feet Interior Design Consultant

Photo: John Stern

and other clerical duties during her 30-hour week, that quota is not always met.

PROMOTION MATERIALS. As part of his program, Ching hired a graphic designer to do the folder or "kit," all materials in it, as well as his stationery and logo. "Since our expertise is interior architecture," he says, "I felt it was wise to get help here and I'm pleased with the results." For $3,500, his firm has a teal-green folder, a four-color graphic description of their services, Ching's biography, client lists, and sheets describing completed projects. All graphic decisions have been made to appeal to the corporate clients the firm is contacting. The consultant also assisted Ching by developing written materials such as the cover letter, press releases, other mailers, and a telephone dialog to assist in making cold calls (which Stein no longer uses, although it was helpful at first, she says).

EVALUATION. Even though Ching

THE SMALL & MEDIUM INDUSTRY BANK (KOREA)

WILL CHING PLANNING & DESIGN was able to achieve for the client, The Small and Medium Industry Bank (Korea), an image that is specifically Korean, (this happens to be the first representative office of the bank outside of Seoul, Korea) while adhering to the rather straightforward interior architectural constraints of the Seagrams Building.

The luminous ceiling, which extends 15 feet from the perimeter wall, dictates the space plan. The color palette, blue/grey with Temple red upholstery accents, is both indigenous to the bank's origins and was selected to compliment the art program acquisitions.

Given a relatively small space to work within, due to the fact that this is only a representative office for the client, the project does reflect a variety of spatial types and functions. Overall privacy is achieved with no sacrifice to good visual communication, which is essential to the operations of an international banking office.

In this design (top) for the Small & Medium Industry Bank (Korea), Ching sought a specifically Korean image within the confines of New York's Seagram Building. Drawing (above) of the same bank is used as a promotional piece that describes the designer's assignment and method of solving the problem.

made use of a written marketing activity program on a timetable and budget, with follow-up for more than a year, the results by 1983 were not encouraging. He estimates a positive response of about 3 percent from the calls. The designated corporate representatives have been the most difficult to reach; Stein has found the architects they've contacted to be the most responsive and the lawyers the least. She puts a carbon of every letter written into a follow-up file. If the phone call two weeks later seems at all positive, she puts that carbon into a "Follow-up in Six Months" file. In mid-1983 they were in the most critical stage of the marketing program. This is when the temptation to give up is the strongest. However, by refining his mailing lists, asking his most sympathetic telephone contacts for further leads, and by persistently following up on them (even sending out more material) Ching feels his goal of a steady supply of work for his small firm will be realized.

Part Two

YOUR MARKETING PLAN

A MARKETING PLAN is the heart of any attempt at focused promoting and selling of design services. Unlike other small businesses, designers almost never record their marketing plan. This is a mistake. Write *something* down. The plan is not a document that must follow a strict or elaborate format to be effective. The ways in which it can be shaped are entirely up to you and your colleagues.

Included in this part of the book are two models for a marketing plan. They try to encompass as many variables as possible that a ten-professional office (more or less the upper limit considered in preparing the book) might want to incorporate. In a sense, they provide a format that even a one-person firm can use. However, it would probably feel like a size 48 man's suit on a size 36 frame. So tailor them.

Writing the marketing plan down has many benefits as you will see. Two of the most significant are, first, that if you record it you can be sure of what you are changing when, in three or six months, it is time for modification. Second, if you keep the various plans that you have made, in time you will begin to see the natural patterns in your firm's business that can be used to *predict* growth and profits. Long-range planning for a design firm is not only possible but extremely desirable.

Chapter Four
SHAPING YOUR MARKETING PLAN

ONCE YOU HAVE analyzed your firm's strengths and weaknesses and set out your marketing goals, you can get on with the more concrete task of creating a marketing plan. In many ways it is as though you have reached the conceptual stage of a design project: you have the program in hand, you know the economic and practical limits of the problem, and now you can dive in. There are many different ways to combine your goals and your business potential. That is, after all, the reason for doing an analysis of your firm and a set of separate goals. Between these two sets of facts (one representing the needs you want to satisfy and the other, the means at your disposal) lies a force field of the imagination that you can use to design a marketing plan exactly suited to your practice.

DESIGNING FOR YOUR NEEDS

AS PAMELA WATERS says: "I'm in business to do what I want to do. If I don't want to do a job, I won't take it. I'm not supporting a fifty-person office so I don't need to take everything. If I'm going to be in business and take all the burdens and responsibilities that go with it, I'm also going to have a good time."

If this statement sounds familiar to you, it is because that's how most designers feel—in their hearts anyway—about running an office. Economic realities, of course, make the achievement of such a practice exceptional rather than commonplace. Yet at the same time, Waters' remark points toward an important potential that marketing holds for designers. It is the means, properly executed, by which you can shape the direction of your practice rather than constantly being forced to take whatever work possibilities come along.

You can see now, if you have in hand an analysis of your firm and its marketing goals, that a series of relationships—as in a "bubble diagram"—can be developed between them. For instance, if one of the obvious strengths of your practice is experience in design of medical facilities or products and an important goal is to increase fees, then continuing to specialize is your path. But if you have been specializing and now your primary goal is diversity, then quite another marketing plan is called for.

A carefully tailored marketing plan is the main advantage of treating process as a design problem. One form of marketing plan was developed

The Marketing Plan

The purpose of a marketing plan is to establish target markets and projected yield for a specified period of time, usually one year. It addresses the organization of the marketing effort and defines responsibilities for its implementation.

A marketing plan generally includes the following:

1. Context. Review and evaluation of previous marketing plans, if any.

2. Markets. Description and analysis of (a) the firm's current markets, services, performance, reputation, and organization; (b) potential future markets; and (c) the overall economic climate for existing and potential markets and factors that may affect them.

3. Capability. A frank assessment of the firm's capability to serve present and potential markets, the firm's competitive position, and its ability to deliver a message and service that is competitive.

4. Goals. A statement of the firm's strategic marketing goals. These may include market specialization or diversification, growth, fee income, profit objectives, sources of work by market, services offered.

5. Marketing organization. Definition of roles and responsibilities for overall direction and management, lead-finding, follow-up activities, maintenance of existing contacts and clients, coordination, administrative support, and so on. Specific assignments should define who will be responsible for which markets, how much time each person will allocate per week or per month, what kind and volume of activity on their part is expected.

6. Marketing tools and resources. A summary of what public relations and promotional tools will be required to implement the plan.

7. Marketing budget. Outline of how much money for personnel time and expenses will be spent on marketing.

8. Market selection and strategies: sales plans. This is the heart of the plan. Market-by-market descriptions of what kind of work will be pursued, the geographic territory, the rationale for the pursuit, the firm's message and distinctive competence, who is responsible, how the work will be pursued (including lead sources), the extent of the effort, in quantifiable and measurable terms, and the projected yield in fees and number of projects.

9. Accountability and control. The system for monitoring and reviewing the plan periodically.

A form of marketing plan outline developed by Carol McConochie lists nine key sections. Designers can adapt such a breakdown to their own special situation. © 1979, 1980 Carol McConochie.

by marketing consultant Carol McConochie and is shown in the box on page 39. Another less formal plan is shown on the right. In the end, however, the form of the marketing plan is far less important than the activity it fosters or inspires. Marketing is about reaching out to people with whom you might otherwise never have the opportunity to work.

BALANCING GOALS AND PRIORITIES

HOWEVER STRONGLY you may wish to pursue your marketing goals, the realities of time and place will dictate the pace of your marketing program. Beside identifying the strengths and weaknesses of your firm, the analytic factors tell you what are the needs that you must meet immediately and in the near future. These become priorities that must be dealt with before marketing can go forward at the pace you now realize it must. There are many limitations on how much energy you can put into looking for work. Most of us have recited them over and over as the reason for not trying to promote and sell at all: not enough time, inadequate cash flow, no one on staff who can help with it, and so on. These and other problems are no doubt apparent in your self-analysis. Yet, once written down, they are more easily dealt with than when they were just shadows—excuses, to be frank—that flitted around in your head. Furthermore, when related to your goals, they no longer seem so formidable and solutions begin to appear.

Joe Jordan and Jim Mitchell, both seasoned in the design business when they became partners, began discussions that led to formation of their firm by analyzing each other's strengths and weaknesses. Then they identified and ranked their joint goals: "We did not formally rank our criteria [goals] but rather considered them as separate components of the mix. If conflict arises, we agree that preserving the firm's reputation for design quality, cost control and client service takes precedence over immediate profitability and growth goals. We do not see any of these goals as mutually incompatible."

For Radford-Biddison, as for many other design firms, the establishment of marketing goals was mixed in with the process of deciding what project categories they were going to go after: specialization was seen as the goal rather than as the means by which more abstract goals could be met. "Our single most important criterion initially was the kind of job," says Gail Biddison. "We wanted to establish ourselves in particular markets like health care or psychiatric facilities to broaden the firm's expertise for a more balanced practice and to increase our depth of experience." In other words they were trying to build credibility and to diversify their business, but without first separating their priorities from clearly defined goals.

In the end, balancing goals and priorities is about helping you decide what is most important in your marketing plan: What do you do first and what second? It is a matter of setting up a hierarchy for planned action.

IDENTIFYING MARKETS

EQUALLY IMPORTANT to the shaping of your plan is deciding who is the audience for your efforts. In other words, where's the work that best fulfills your goals? Ralph Appelbaum, for example, has found two rather different markets that fit his criteria. For a number of years he has worked primarily for museums, which operate on public funds and in the public trust, doing scientific exhibit

---

Elements of a Marketing Plan

This is a plan for design services, not for a product or such other services as construction management or real estate development.

Goals Statement (Part 1) *
1. Clearly stated and defined
2. Ranked if possible (optional)

Overall Marketing Program
1. Statement of purpose
2. Geographic constraints
3. Economic constraints

Various Identified Markets with Description of Each (Part 2)
1. Statement of market (who, what, why)
2. Geographic particulars
3. Market's size and potential for growth
4. Expected share and "edge" in that market
5. How each market will be pursued (Chapter 10)
   a. By whom and how hard
   b. Techniques
   c. Time framework
   d. Fee proposals

Overall Administration or Marketing Control (Part 3)
1. Meetings (frequency)
2. Who's in charge
3. Updating of plan (frequency)
4. Expectations of firm from marketers
5. Economic projections based on marketing program

Budget
1. Amount available (all this is overhead) (Part 3)
   a. Principals' time/salaries
   b. Marketing support time/ salaries
   c. Materials
   d. Postage
   e. Telephone
   f. Travel and entertainment
2. Accounting for time and expenses

*References are to parts and chapters in this book that explain each topic.

A STRATEGIC PLAN

FOR KOSTER AND HOLZHEIMER ARCHITECTS INC.

INTRODUCTION

Preparation of a strategic plan is a giant step forward. For the first time, our firm's future will be mapped out, its hopes pinned to a plan reduced to writing. This plan will be invested with an intelligence that gears action to strategy. Above all, it will:

. Provide us with a vision of the ways in which we can fulfill our highest potential as architects.

. Help us to survive, grow, and compete in the architectural marketplace.

. Help us make a better life for ourselves, our families, and our communities a reality.

One word of caution, however. A strategic plan is not a template that we can place over our firm and stamp out performance. Nor is it a piece of machinery or a "quick fix" for whatever may ail our firm. Rather, it is a concept, a method, a process that works. But it does not work automatically or by itself. Only we, as officers of the firm, can make it work. Only we can breathe life into the plan.

Unfolding below is a first effort at setting our goals and drafting a strategy to meet them. So we can expect lapses in logic and errors in judgment to slip into our plan. But with each succeeding effort, made yearly, we expect our strategic planning to improve steadily.

Koster and Holzheimer recognize, in this preamble to their strategic plan, that the goals and the marketing process itself will evolve as they work at developing new business.

design. Recently his firm has begun to design for corporations in the health and energy fields, especially those serving the public interest through advanced technology. Although the two client types operate on quite a different basis, from Appelbaum's point of view they are equally interesting. Understandably, each requires a different marketing approach. The discreet, scholarly technique Appelbaum has used with museums in the past will be inadequate in this new area. He is now restructuring his office from an atelier-style operation to one with a compartmentalized format as a prelude to creating more focused business development strategies.

In Koster and Holzheimer's Strategic Plan drawn up in 1982, they pose seven questions as a means for identifying their markets, which are shown in the accompanying box. These questions led directly to a three-market program (recreation centers, libraries, and municipal facilities) that covers a 200-mile radius from Cleveland, mainly to the southern and western parts of Ohio. Then the program was further developed and approved by the K & H Board of Directors.

EXAMINING A MARKETING PLAN

WHEN YOU COME right down to it, a marketing plan is not the formidable document that business mythology has made it. When you read of how high-powered marketing consultants approach corporate or even real estate development projects, it seems as though some kind of magic is being pulled off. In fact, any marketing plan—no matter how complicated it may look—answers the seven questions posed in the accompanying box.

The best plans are based upon thorough market research involving consultants. But before a discussion of the role of consultants and reference books, the important point is that even a modest, one-page plan is better than nothing, as long as it gives you the guidance to begin seeking new business in a logical manner. Every plan, after all, should evolve and grow more complex as you research your markets and as you learn by contacting potential clients.

Of the design firms interviewed in this book, Jaffe Acoustics is among the furthest along on a structured marketing program. Ann Boyar, JAI's marketing director, prepared its first formal plan late in 1982. The seventeen-page document is somewhat more complex than a standard design services marketing plan because it includes seven pages devoted to Electronic Reflected Energy System (ERES) and Boardroom (two electronic acoustical supplement concepts that Jaffe intended to franchise at the time). The sections devoted to general marketing are complete in themselves. They contain the elements shown in the box on page 44.

As of mid-1983, the ideas for an up-dated brochure and increased new business contacts were moving slowly, but the newsletter program (for example see page 142) had taken off quite handsomely. In her quarterly reviews of the marketing plan, Boyar has made adjustments for changes in the economy and the firm's business circumstances as time passes.

USING REFERENCE BOOKS AND CONSULTANTS

OUR MAILBOXES offer abundant help in learning about marketing design services. Those who have books, newsletters, seminars, and other resources to sell use direct mail to reach approximately one-quarter of a million U.S. design professionals.

1. What are our markets?

2. What is the size of each market?

3. What share of each market will we have?

4. What is each market's potential for growth?

5. How can we best satisfy each market?

6. How should we price our architectural (design) services so as to make a fair profit while remaining competitive?

7. What is our place or "edge" in these markets?

Basic Marketing Issues

Why do you want more business?

What do you have to offer?

Where are your markets?

How are you going to tap them?

Who is going to do the work?

When do you expect results?

What is the program going to cost?

Since any such purchase is deductible from income taxes as a valid professional expense, it makes sense to acquire as many of these aids as you can productively use. Often the seminars and books are offered at a discount through your professional design organization. These are likely to be especially valuable because the content should be focused on your particular discipline by the sponsors. Marketing newsletters are available that give tips on strategies and planning as well as case studies that may be applicable to promoting and selling your practice's services.

Consultants who offer professional marketing services for designers (see accompanying box) have organized for advancement of their specialty. The Society for Marketing Professional Services (SMPS) has chapters in cities throughout the country, some of which hold monthly meetings with speakers who discuss aspects of promoting and selling design services. The name of a contact person in your city or region can be obtained by writing or calling the SMPS national offices in Alexandria, Virginia. *Professional Services Management Journal* also offers an annual list of management and marketing consultants who specialize in serving design firms (see also box).

Consultant Names and Addresses (Partial list)

Ernest Burden
Ernest Burden Associates
20 Waterside Plaza
New York City 10010
(212) 889-4672

Joan Capelin or Ann Landreth
Capelin & Landreth, Inc.
229 East 60th Street
New York City 10022
(212) 421-1900

Weld Coxe
The Coxe Group, Inc.
Two Girard Plaza
Philadelphia, PA 19102
(215) 561-2020

Robert B. Darling
The MGI Management
Institute
Two East Avenue
Larchmont, NY 10538
(914) 834-8798

Gerre Jones
Gerre Jones Associates, Inc.
P.O. Box 32387
Washington, D.C. 20007
(202) 333-2366 or 965-1740

Barbara Beck Lord
Lord Communications
134 Beach Street
Boston, MA 02111
(617) 451-9475

Carol McConochie
McConochie Consulting
312 South Camac Street
Philadelphia, PA 19107
(215) 735-3744

Dr. Stuart W. Rose, AIA
Professional Development
Resources, Inc.
1000 Connecticut Avenue
N.W., Suite Nine
Washington D.C. 20036
(202) 362-0800

Frank Stasiowski, AIA
Practice Management
Associates, Ltd.
126 Harvard Street
Brookline, MA 02146
(617) 731-1912

David Travers
1119 Colorado Avenue
Santa Monica, CA 90401
(213) 395-8732 or 393-5230

Organizations

Design Management Institute
Massachusetts College of Art
364 Brookline Avenue
Boston, MA 02115
(617) 731-2340

Harvard Graduate School of Design
Gund Hall 503
Cambridge, MA 02138
(617) 495-9340
Three-day summer seminar,
"Marketing Tools
and Tactics for Design
Offices."

Professional Development Programs
The American Institute of
Architects
1735 New York Avenue N.W.
Washington D.C. 20006
(202) 626-7354

Professional Services Management Journal (PSMJ)
P.O. Box 11316
Newington, CT 06111
(203) 666-9487

Society for Marketing Professional Services (SMPS) News
1437 Powhatan Street
Alexandria, VA 22314
(703) 549-6117

Beside books and articles on marketing, the most cost- and time-effective method for learning about new business development is the one- to three-day seminar held regularly in major cities in the United States by professional organizations and other sponsors. Seminars offer a double benefit to those who attend: First you experience an intense exposure to the subject of marketing taught by knowledgeable people in a short period. Second, you have the opportunity to mingle with your peers when classes are not in session and have the sort of nuts-and-bolts discussions that sometimes mean more in the long run than the formal meetings. These seminars will cost you $200 per day on average.

The one shortcoming, for many designers, of the books and seminars offered today is that they are focused on techniques and programs that are often too elaborate and expensive to be easily applied to a small practice. However, informal sessions with others from offices of ten professionals or less can be a side benefit of seminars. Promotion and sales principles themselves do not change drastically when practiced on a small budget—they just demand more energy and time from those who must keep the firm going and look for more work at the same time. Nobody said it was easy.

COST ACCOUNTING AND MARKETING

ONE OF THE MOST valuable tools a designer can have when preparing a marketing plan is to know what it cost his or her firm to produce the jobs already completed. Not only does this provide enormous support when negotiating fees (see section on Negotiating, on page 119), but it helps to identify specialties or areas of practice where the fees justify your efforts. You may not decide on which areas to concentrate based on profitability alone, but it helps to clarify your planning when such facts are available. Two sources to help you keep track of your firm's finances are *A Guide to Business Principles and Practices for Interior Designers* by Harry Siegel, CPA, and *Financial Management for Design Professionals* by Lowell Getz, CPA, and Frank Stasiowski, AIA.

Judith Chafee and Infield + D'Astolfo, both very small firms, have found that the more detailed accounting methods used to keep track of individual jobs helps as well with marketing. Basically, that means keeping closer track of time spent by you, the principal, in getting things going and completing them on time. Even if drafters and secretaries keep good time records, it is not unusual for the boss, running around from job to job and doing a dozen different things in a day, to fail to do so. It's true it is hard to find those few minutes before closing up shop to divide up your time among current projects. But it is perhaps the most valuable single gift you can give yourself in the long run.

How it works in shaping the marketing plan is that you assemble and analyze comparative cost statements for every job completed in the past two or three years. Using their microcomputer, Jordan/Mitchell can call forth that sort of data quickly and concisely, since they have entered all such information into the system. But just because you may not have that electronic capability as yet, do not despair. It is a function of standard bookkeeping analysis that can be found in any accounting text. The important point is that when your recent design accomplishments are viewed solely from the profit-or-loss point of view, a pattern that may be quite surprising will emerge: Work you like to do may prove to be very unprofitable because you spend too much time on it. Thus, when you choose those areas for marketing emphasis, you will at least be aware of the potential consequences.

Jaffe Marketing Plan Highlights

1. A descriptive table of contents

2. Today's economy and what it means to us
   a. Four markets (new performing arts centers; theater renovation; convention centers and arenas; pavilions, tents, and shells)
   b. A marketing approach for each

3. Overall marketing plan and implementation
   a. Leads and follow-up
   b. Feasibility studies
   c. New contacts
   d. Brochures and advertisements

4. Target dates and tasks (three months, nine months, fifteen months)

5. Proposed annual budget

THE ART OF
MARKETING "DIVERSITY"

IT IS MORE DIFFICULT to build a marketing plan around variety than around specialization. Furthermore, a major reason why designers shy away from formal marketing techniques is because they fear that this discipline will put them in a creative straitjacket. In fact a creative designer can use those same design abilities to produce a responsive, flexible marketing program.

Gere Kavanaugh, like Pamela Waters, has built her practice around "things I like to do." Each practices a broad-based, inventive approach to design that ranges across several traditional design categories. Each does special parts of a bigger job when given a chance—the part that people remember. Both, incidentally, are dramatic, dynamic women who seem not to worry very much about presenting the dignified, even staid appearance that so many male designers feel is required. Thus, as a solution to the dilemma of selling "diversity," celebrate your exuberance rather than try to explain it to potential clients.

There is a strong and continuing trend away from the minimalist approach that modern architecture brought to all design fields. Thus promotional materials that use techniques from retail advertising no longer startle people. Big and powerful typefaces, bright colors, splashy forms, stunning and unexpected photographs can all be combined to sweep the prospect off his or her feet. Or out of your office, if such personal expressiveness doesn't appeal to that individual.

An integral part of shaping your marketing plan, therefore, is knowing who your audience is. That can mean knowing who the audience is in emotional terms as well as the more quantitative ones. For instance, by basing your marketing research on the techniques that cosmetic companies or popular music producers use—studying the results of their polls (published in trade journals and familiar to public relations and marketing counselors) and applying them to your own ends—you could create a unique promotion campaign. Such imaginative approaches allow you to focus your marketing efforts confidently in directions other design firms might hesitate to follow.

But there is also a pragmatic basis for the approach that Kavanaugh and Waters have taken. Their designs make money for clients. Why not a marketing approach based on the economic advantages of fresh, lively design? Find out how your past projects have paid off. Get solid figures and build case studies around improved earnings in a renovated retail space, for instance, or increased sales of a redesigned product. The combination of vivid design with a record of income-producing results is a mighty effective way to sell your services.

SELECTING
YOUR CLIENTS

MARKETING IS ABOUT finding people who want what you've got to sell. The more people who find out about your firm and its work, the more likely you are to come across people whom you'd choose to work for.

"Our number one goal is the ability to do our type of work," says Edward Mills of Voorsanger and Mills. "That means having the freedom to do the kind of designs that are consonant with our esthetic philosophy." Publication in many journals has brought Voorsanger and Mills attention that most designers only dream of receiving. As a result the quality of projects (and size of budgets) offered them has increased dramatically. And yet the firm's desire to maintain a well-rounded practice is jeopardized by the success of their elaborate post-modern interiors. Their fortunate situation (high visibility, a growing staff, steady workload) offers a marketing opportunity nonetheless. By capitalizing on it they can go looking for the large-scale architectural projects they want, free to decide which projects they accept. It's a nice position to be in.

Yet any vigorous marketing program can offer those benefits. Whenever you have more than enough work to keep the wolf away from the door, the fear of imminent disaster recedes and you can say "no" to jobs you would rather avoid. *The problem is that, just when they gain this precious marketing advantage, most designers stop prospecting.*

By drawing up a long-range plan, anticipating the possibility after a year or two of much more work coming in, you can be prepared to increase staff size as required and keep from being so swamped that you can't maintain your promotional impetus. The value of intense marketing, of being considered for lots of jobs—don't worry, you won't get them all!—is that you can select the ones you would really like, putting extra effort into those presentations. For the prospects you are less enchanted with, you can always quote a higher than normal fee. Chances are, if you're feeling confident, you'll get it!

LEARNING
"THE HARD WAY"

ANOTHER OPTION, one to be embraced with great caution, is to learn by experience. "I've gotten very little from books and those kinds of sources," says Gordon Perry. "I find, perhaps it's my nature, that I've had to learn everything the hard way about marketing. Try it, do it, see if it works, and then try again."

Al De Vido is another person who has learned about marketing "the hard way." He has flirted with the idea of structured marketing but has never pursued it. Like Voorsanger and Mills, he hasn't had to. His small, mainly single-family house practice has prospered because of extensive publication. Yet he is not satisfied with the way things are going. DeVido, like so many other designers, would like to diversify his practice. What to do? In his handsome portfolio are pages showing offices, retail stores, theater renovations, and other interesting projects along with what seem like dozens of houses. Here is a case where a simple marketing plan, aimed at one or two of the areas he has already worked in, could broaden his practice within a year or two if he chooses to pursue it vigorously.

You too can go on doing it "the hard way." After all, that's how most of us learned the business in the offices where we trained: Hire when help is needed, fire when it isn't. However, marketing is a way to break the endless cycle of financial feast and famine that small design offices, especially, are subject to.

Chapter Five
RECORDING
YOUR PLAN

LOOKING FOR new business without a plan or without writing the plan down is a little bit like designing a house on the back of an envelope and using that sketch to construct it. Yet those designers who bother to think through an approach for finding more work often resist putting it down on paper. Perhaps they feel the statement will limit their flexibility or will inhibit the easy-going spirit that a design firm is supposed to have. Don't worry, even more than design sketches, marketing plans are meant to change—three or four times a year if necessary. They should be short and simple, easy to read, and easy to modify. Six double-spaced, typed pages may be enough to do the job for you—ten for sure.

WRITING IT DOWN
MAKES A DIFFERENCE

FEW OF THE sixteen designers represented in this book actually have a written marketing plan. Some of the rest, also quite serious about going after new jobs, feel that, like the Constitution of Great Britain, it is best left as a goal in itself. However, writing it down can make a difference.

The marketing plan is a tool. It is one thing to imagine a beautiful hammer, quite another to drive home a nail with it. There are several reasons why a written marketing plan ought to precede the expensive or at least time-consuming efforts that are described in the following sections of this book, including the preparation of promotional materials.

First, putting the plan into words helps shape and clarify your promotional and selling ideas. If one partner is assigned the task of writing it down, then the others can respond to the specifics rather than tossing vaguely understood concepts and business-school cliches back and forth year after year.

Second, a written plan can be referred to as needed and marked up as one or another person doing the calls or going to interviews has a new thought about the firm's procedures.

Third, as subsequent plans are developed, the older ones can be pulled from the file for instructive comparison. We keep yellow tracing paper sketches for years, don't we? Why not keep a record of business intentions to set against the account books as a way of measuring the actual business history by what we sought through marketing development.

Fourth, it is terribly easy to lose sight of task assignments and deadlines for accomplishing them when there is no record. Prospecting efforts must be reduced to step-by-step directions or no action will ever be taken. The stated plan serves as an agenda in the reporting sessions that a firm committed to marketing must hold every week or two if any success is to result.

To write down a marketing plan costs almost nothing. If you could hire a consultant to advise you on business development, one of the benefits you would expect for the fees you pay are reports and graphics stating the expert's recommendations. Why not do them for yourself? The only requirement is the cost of the typing and an hour or so of drafting time.

PUTTING IT IN
PLAIN LANGUAGE

FOR THE MARKETING plan to serve all the functions just noted and to be understood by everyone in the office, use clear, straightforward language. If you've seen professionally prepared marketing plans, you may have been impressed by the authoritative quality of the language, the length and the complexity of the presentation. That's fine for a corporation or even for a large design firm that deals with corporate clients. For most designers, the object is to create a plan that will inspire marketing action rather than impress people. Here are some suggestions:

1. Most important, avoid business jargon. Instead of: "Gross income generation potential for fiscal year 1984 based on current market projections appears to be $357,527.43." Write: "We expect $358,000 total income in 1984." There are some basic terms, however, such as "marketing plan," "profitability," "cold calls," and a few others that are the easiest way to describe the idea. If it would be helpful, define the word in parentheses immediately following your first use of it.

2. Use the present tense whenever possible rather than the future or the conditional. Instead of writing, "Next year we will try to make a minimum of three cold calls each week." Or: "We would like to propose for the next year that three cold calls per week be targeted." Write: "Three cold calls per week is our objective next year."

3. Always work for short, simple sentences. If you find that a sentence has two or three clauses and more than twenty-five words in it, go back and look for ways to break it into two or three units. The previous sentence has thirty-three words in it. It can also be written this way: Does the sentence have two or more clauses? More than twenty-five words? Then look for ways to subdivide it. Now it uses twenty-one words; the ideas are also easier to understand.

4. Be specific. Don't write: "The field of interior renovation offers a number of possibilities that the firm may wish to explore as potential project development sources such as institutional uses, commercial and retail facilities, public assembly areas." Instead, "Interior renovation project possibilities are nursing homes, publishing offices, butcher shops, hiring halls."

5. Aim for a positive and upbeat tone. The idea is to turn your colleagues on to marketing, not to emphasize its difficulty or long-term nature. Avoid: "It's not going to be easy, but we have to try to meet these cold telephone call quotas as best we can." Instead: "Let's work together on these cold calls. That way we can easily meet the quota."

6. Use graphic devices such as descriptive headlines, underlining, or bullets to draw attention to the main points you want your readers to absorb. Lists and tables are a better way to organize statistics than sentences. The optimal layout gives each item appropriate emphasis while keeping the overall statement as compact as possible.

The need for effective language skills in all aspects of design is something that most designers discover only after they leave school. However, it is an issue that is crucial in promotion and sales work. That is because you are dealing with potential clients who use the language for entirely different purposes than do the people in your firm. Both have to understand what is going on for marketing to be successful. A good source of information about using language skills in the design field is *Creative Communications for a Successful Design Practice* by Stephen A. Kliment, FAIA. For a thorough analysis of the English language aimed at more effective writing and speaking in general read *The Art of Plain Talk* by Rudolph Flesch.

SETTING YOUR OBJECTIVES

THE OPERATING PART of a marketing plan is the section that spells out how each of the identified markets will be pursued by the firm. It is the chart where your short-term objectives and the time framework in which they will be carried out are listed (see accompanying box).

In the marketing report she prepared for Jaffe Acoustics Inc., Ann Boyar included a page titled "Target Dates and Tasks." She notes that these responsibilities are "beyond the normal ongoing marketing tasks with leads, follow-ups, etc." Then she sets out three time periods: three months after issuing the plan, the next six months, six more months, bringing the total time frame to fifteen months. Under each time period she lists the marketing objectives or tasks in order of priority, including a brief description of the work to be done. There is also space left for notation of progress made as time passes.

The chart on page 51 sets up a marketing program that specifies the techniques to be applied to each of your chosen markets (see page 102 for a detailed description of the tasks). It assumes several different markets, each with one of your partners in charge. The various objectives may well be carried out only by that individual or with the help of one or two marketing support people. The form also allows many people on the staff to be involved, a distribution of marketing duties that is highly desirable.

> ### *Marketing Objectives*
>
> **What** are you going to do?
>
> **How** are you going to do it?
>
> **Who** is responsible?
>
> **When** will it be done?

UPDATING TO KEEP IT VIGOROUS

THE MORE ELABORATE the charts and procedures, the more likely the marketing plan will end up on the shelf. It's not clear why overdesign in certain situations has the effect of drying up the spontaneous energies previously active there. That is a problem you may encounter if you attempt to establish a marketing program that is too ambitious for your resources.

On the other hand, there is Judith Chafee's experience: "Our plans are simply responses to opportunities. They change often." A perception that Ralph Appelbaum seconded in virtually the same words. Yet a totally ad hoc approach to looking for new work is what designers have always practiced and it isn't good enough. Warren Infield describes a somewhat more structured approach: "We revise our plan when we become convinced that our current plan is not producing results." Radford-Biddison's approach seems to strike a good balance between the extremes: "We now take time out about every three to six months to assess how successful marketing particular areas has been. At the same time we decide how successful our recently completed jobs have been in terms of financial and personal satisfaction."

The answer to having a plan that works for you rather than forcing you to work for it is frequent updating and modification. In the first year of serious marketing, you may well want to restructure your activities every three months to learn from the lessons that actual contacts with prospects have taught you. By adjusting your methods—such as redoubling telephone efforts if a mailing campaign has not borne fruit—in the light of your original goals, you can rekindle the enthusiasm of those pursuing the marketing program with you. After all, the intention of organized marketing for designers is to focus your colleagues' natural energies toward finding new clients, not to smother or frustrate them.

PLANNING SHORT- AND LONG-TERM STRATEGIES

ACCORDING TO Gordon Perry: "My plan runs maybe for six months and then I try to revise it because the business climate changes so rapidly. My experience in the design profession changes in an interesting way too—synergistically. For instance, I didn't plan to do sporting goods until I got such an account. Now I'm looking for other sporting equipment manufacturers. And since I had to go to Taiwan for this client, I'm considering doing more work there. Even so, all of this fits into my fifteen-year long-range plan. I'm looking to establish myself as a recognized designer, be able to find profitable jobs easier and then concentrate on work that I can really sink my teeth into—the kind of research and design exploration that I feel is so important."

The necessity for marketing *goals* becomes more apparent when you think about your practice on a long-term basis. What do you want to have accomplished in five years? In ten years? Koster's firm is an example of that kind of planning. "We have a five-year plan that is revised every year and modified every six months by our Board of Directors—at their insistence. I learned from my banker how to make three-year income and expense projections. He got me to look at the long term rather than the immediate economic picture. He taught me the value and the discipline of cash-flow projections. Now, based on our marketing plan I can predict the number of projects, potential gross income, staff requirements and thus project our profit goals for the next half-decade."

Don't just mull over these long-range thoughts when you're driving back from a client meeting. It is just as important to record them as it is to write down your weekly prospecting results.

Short-Term Strategies

1. Pursue job possibilities vigorously in your marketing area through research, calls, letters, canvassing, and follow-up.

2. Build credibility through publication, publicity, and advertising in local publications.

3. Keep in touch with former clients and friends through regular periodic communications.

4. Think through your presentation techniques and promotional materials in terms of your present marketing program.

5. Commit your marketing efforts to paper, keep track of their effectiveness, and update the plan frequently.

Long-Term Strategies

1. Study regional and national economic projections for trends that will affect your professional choices.

2. Develop specialties that reflect long-term demographic trends.

3. Plan professional and support staff development based on each individual's growth potential.

4. Construct a three-year cash-flow projection based on both optimistic and pessimistic workload scenarios with help from an accountant.

5. Determine the amount or percentage of profit the firm should aim for over the next five years.

MHD

1984 MARKETING PROGRAM OBJECTIVES
MICKEY. HICKEY + DICKEY · INDUSTRIAL DESIGNERS

MARKET	PARTNER-IN-CHARGE	MARKETING OBJECTIVES	TIME FRAMEWORK
		COLD TELEPHONE CALLS	
		GENERAL LETTERS	
		PERSONAL LETTERS	
		BROCHURE/COVER LETT.	
		FOLLOW UP LETTERS	
		CANVASSING VISITS	
		INTERVIEWS	

MARKET	PARTNER-IN-CHARGE	MARKETING OBJECTIVES	TIME FRAMEWORK
		COLD TELEPHONE CALLS	
		GENERAL LETTERS	

MARKET	PARTNER-IN-CHARGE	MARKETING OBJECTIVES	TIME FRAMEWORK
		COLD TELEPHONE CALLS	

In order to sustain adequate momentum during the early months of your program, you may find that a chart which spells out the assignments of each staff member will be helpful.

Chapter Six
CONSIDERING SPECIAL CIRCUMSTANCES

THE DESIGN DISCIPLINES included in this book have a great deal in common, especially when it comes to looking for new work. But each design practice is also a business shaped by its owners in response to unique circumstances. Four considerations, derived in part from the experience of designers participating here, are discussed in this chapter. There are many more adjustments that you, as you read through the material that follows, may want to make in this marketing process.

One consideration that receives no direct attention elsewhere in the book is the way that styles of doing business vary from one region of the United States to another. From the tightly structured commerce in the biggest cities of the northeast to the laid-back style of the mushrooming Sunbelt metropolises, there are significant differences in business customs. If you practice in a small town or a predominantly rural area, many of the ideas noted here will seem almost rude in their assertiveness. It is up to you how you adapt them to your needs.

DEALING WITH A LIMITED MARKET

THE MARKETING programs outlined in the next part of the book are based mainly on architectural and interior design practice. They are necessary for two reasons: First the jobs being sought are frequently large and complex, with commissions awarded only after thorough review of competing designers by committees or corporate boards. Second these prospects often have so little in common with each other as businesses that it is difficult to group them into "markets" in the traditional sense of the word. The requirement for elaborate reporting systems so necessary to marketing by architects and interior designers may, therefore, be irrelevant to other disciplines.

Ken Arutunian, for instance, who heads a small landscape design firm in Palo Alto, does not do residential work. He has little need to reach out to "the public" in his prospecting efforts. The market, as he sees it, is large architectural and engineering firms in the Bay Area that normally hire landscape architects as consultants or subcontractors. To a lesser extent, his firm looks for park and recreation work from nearby cities and counties. In both cases, the number of contacts is finite—in fact limited enough so that today he could probably identify the organizations and key personnel that make up more than 90 percent of his total market. A situation like that calls for a much more specific marketing plan than is usual.

Jaffe Acoustics is a design consulting firm, on the other hand, that services a national market. However focused it may be in terms of potential theater renovations and concert halls, the prospecting must cover dozens of cities. In 1982 Jaffe planned to market and franchise two electronic acoustic devices; much of the firm's marketing commitment reflected that aspect of its business.

Small engineering offices have similar marketing profiles to those of AKA and Jaffe Acoustics. For example, if a small mechanical engineering firm chooses to focus on a single city or region as its work area, the prospecting efforts are relatively straight-forward. A well-written prospecting letter sent to local architects and contractors should generate quite a few solid leads, especially if the level of regional construction activity is reasonably high. Larger engineering organizations often have half-a-dozen corporate-type architectural firms as clients, a good base on which to build. But subsequent marketing efforts may require elaborate development in order to find work in the national marketplace.

In disciplines like graphic design and residential interior design, where it is customary to build the fee into the total delivered cost of a job, the marketing process differs from those design fields that only offer services. For one thing, "price" can be an extremely important issue in selling, which naturally affects the way you market. For the second, many of the prospects are first-time buyers. "We spend a good deal of time," says Warren Infield, "educating smaller clients, trying to establish a decent budget with people unaccustomed to the cost of quality printing—not always a profitable way to spend our time."

MATCHING EFFORTS TO YOUR FIRM'S SIZE

As a design firm grows from the truly small category (one principal and up to three staff members or two principals and no staff) toward multiple partners and associates, as in the case of Jeanne Hartnett's office, marketing becomes a more formal process: if only because individuals have less and less opportunity to keep in touch on new business prospects. In the case of her Chicago office with four principals, serious promotion and selling began with the perception that they had to reach out to the Sunbelt. Because the economy in their former region of operations had slowed so markedly, they resolved at the same time to do a spiral-bound brochure that would emphasize the breadth of their expertise. The book in turn led to development of a cover letter-and-brochure promotion campaign. There was no date on which a planned marketing program began. It evolved as the firm grew and needed to find more work.

UDA Architects reached the four-partner stage without any marketing plan, relying instead on a consistent weekly partners' meeting to handle their prospecting needs. On the other hand, Pam Radford and Gail Biddison began their small interiors firm with a several-month analysis of potential markets for their new joint enterprise. In other words, it is never too early to begin thinking about creating a marketing program.

WHEN YOU CHANGE YOUR OPERATIONS

SOMETIMES A substantial change in the way you do business offers an opportunity to set up a marketing program—or at least to reconsider the way you have gone about it in the past. Rapid growth in staff size is an obvious example. Ralph

Appelbaum has seen his office grow to nine people in less than three years on the strength of referrals alone. He first began thinking about actively promoting it in mid-1983.

A common problem that can equally inhibit fast growth in marketing is lack of adequate capital; the cash-flow situation may dictate a very modest program. But almost anyone can afford to make a few phone calls or write some letters each week.

Opening a new branch office, entering a joint venture, or acquiring an existing practice in another specialty requires promotion and sales planning as well. In fact, do not enter into any such financial commitment without working out the new business possibilities *beforehand*. A small design business starting out in one place can muddle along for years, avoiding bankruptcy by the narrowest of margins. When sudden growth or increase in its operations occurs based on apparently substantial contractual arrangements, potentially disastrous financial vulnerability is introduced. That is when the benefits of sound business management, of which marketing is a central component, come to the fore.

Ironic as it may seem, too much work coming unexpectedly can generate as severe economic stress within your practice as not enough. Suppose a big job comes in unexpectedly. You staff up, begin design preliminaries, and then realize you can't afford to carry this expanded payroll until the first payment is received from the client. A continuing marketing program that includes projections of future staff, cash-flow, and other requirements may not anticipate such developments. The existence of an even rudimentary financial plan, however, gives you a broader basis on which to decide how to incorporate the new business into your existing workload than no plan at all. That can make the difference between smooth growth and just another hire-and-fire fiasco.

TEACHING AS MARKETING

DESIGN, MORE perhaps than most professions, has close ties to the academic world. It is common, especially among small offices, for people to teach and practice simultaneously. In the early days of a practice, of course, teaching is a good way to pay the rent on your studio. But that is not the main reason most designers teach. The commitment to student growth and development, of nurturing the future of the profession, is generally a sincere one.

Ralph Appelbaum returned, a few years ago, to teach in the Industrial Design Department at Pratt Institute, his alma mater. He found it, as time went on, an excellent way as well to build his staff with the best members of each class. As his practice has matured, moreover, he has decided to use teaching in a more productive fashion. Now he lectures on exhibition design to graduate and postgraduate students in New York University's Museum Studies Program. These people later become the same curators who commission designers to work on their projects. Teaching is marketing in this case.

Judith Chafee and Will Ching see design teaching as having strong promotional value. Chafee is Adjunct Professor of Architecture at the University of Arizona. She finds that her academic position, along with continuing publication in national magazines, is the "major source of security for prospective clients." Ching, another Pratt alumnus, has served as a thesis critic in its Interior Design Department for several years. He has found that his "sense of design has been revitalized by talking so intensely about it with students." In return, when he has shared that with potential clients, he has also been able to inspire them.

Both Warren Infield and Frank D'Astolfo teach and lecture. They find it provides "a certain prestige and credibility with potential clients." However, since so much graphic design is done on tight schedules they have learned that teaching is an activity that must be kept in proper perspective since "clients expect our constant attention." Infield found, during periods when he was teaching full time, that potential clients often gave large-scale projects to "working professionals" instead of to him. As a result, he feels it is important for those who teach to maintain a businesslike image for their practice.

A teaching position will limit both the amount of practice and the amount of prospecting that a designer can do. Firms such as Voorsanger and Mills and UDA find that the prestige of having a partner teach at Columbia and Yale, respectively, is worth the time it takes away from the office. If your firm has academic connections, make the most of them in your marketing program.

Things to Do

Read what experts on marketing have to say and follow their advice as you shape and carry out your plan.

Attend local marketing seminars and talk over your problems with your peers.

Stick to your stated goals as you shape the marketing plan but keep it flexible should your goals change.

Include an operating statement (individual responsibilities, quotas, and reporting dates) in every plan.

Incorporate the unique aspects of your firm in your plan.

Review your cost accounting records as a way of identifying profitable and money-losing services or specialties in your practice.

Begin making three-year (or longer) projections of staff needs, cash-flow, and project loads based on your plan.

Always keep in mind your audience: Who is your market?

Things to Avoid

Learning about marketing "the hard way"—no plan, no structure, no records.

Ignoring the realities and limits presented by self-analysis of your firm.

Being timid about pushing forward your firm's obvious strengths.

Including complicated, jargon-stuffed language in your written plan.

Looking for a formula approach to business planning: It may not fit your needs.

Plans that are too ambitious for your financial capability right now or too complicated.

Plans that inhibit *in any way* the natural desire of your colleagues to go out and get work for the firm.

Alfredo De Vido Associates, Architects

699 Madison Avenue,
New York City 10021

Single-family residences
contract interior design
some commercial and
institutional projects

Established: 1978

Educational Background:
B. Arch., Carnegie-Mellon;
M.F.A., Princeton;
Dipl., Town Planning, Royal Academy
of Fine Arts, Copenhagen

Professional Society:
American Institute of Architects

Alfredo De Vido

PROFESSIONAL FRAMEWORK. If anyone profiled here has a "dream practice," at least to another architect, it is Alfredo De Vido. He works from a small, elegantly detailed office on Manhattan's Upper East Side designing mostly handsome single-family houses, each appropriate to its owners' needs and to its site. Interviews with prospects, who read about him in magazines or find him through one of his former clients, take about three or four hours of De Vido's time every week. He does little formalized marketing otherwise. Yet his is a well-run office by any standard. "Our budget/schedule skills are good," De Vido says. "Part of our success has been the ability to come close on small budgets. We manage the subs well and compare favorably with other professionals who aim for a high design level. In fact, our major strength seems to be good, talented personnel who are attracted to the firm by our reputation."

GOALS AND OBJECTIVES. A steady flow of work into his office has made the setting of marketing goals a low priority for De Vido. Even so, he has

a continuing interest in broadening the kinds of work his firm does. "I do not neglect houses, realizing that they are a continuing source of income and satisfaction. However, they are not very profitable and it is necessary to exercise careful cost control and discipline to make money on them." That may be why he wants to find other kinds of projects. He already has completed a considerable number of stores, offices, and performing arts centers. The centers were done when De Vido was in a former partnership, but the other work came from people for whom he first did a house. He could well set up a marketing program for one or two of those specialties. Like most designers who have a strong referral operation going, De Vido has never needed other work so he has not gone after it.

MARKETING STRATEGY. Although De Vido does not have a formal marketing program, he has sought professional assistance in the past. A marketing consultant proposed that if he sought work on a larger scale than houses, he would need to

expand his firm in some fashion, either with partners or by adding associates in a joint venture in order to convince clients of his capacity to handle the work. De Vido was also urged to focus on prestige jobs, contacting cultural leaders through influential people for whom he worked. He has also read books but finds "most of the advice contained therein is aimed at larger firms. The main problem they posed was making the leap from a small firm to a large firm." De Vido, like most of the other principals profiled in this book, does not want to have a lot of employees; he just wants to do bigger and more interesting jobs.

PROMOTION MATERIAL. In spite of his "nonmarketer" attitude, De Vido has developed promotional literature that is both elegant and complete. In addition to tearsheets of the dozen or more articles that appear each year on his houses (many are in glossy Japanese and German magazines), he has developed—and keeps up to date—a series of project description sheets (see examples on page 141) that might serve as models of quality for even the largest design firm. Another promotion tool for De Vido is his books, *Designing Your Client's House,* published in 1983, and *Houses/Stores/Offices: Designing and Managing Small Projects,* to be issued in 1984, both of which will further establish his reputation as a top business-conscious professional.

EVALUATION. De Vido's custom of sending off packages of his latest tearsheets to former clients is an effective yet economical tactic. But otherwise he avoids self-promotion— not even a follow-up letter after a potential client has come into his office to discuss a house. With his elegant promotional materials, he is fully prepared—if he wants bigger jobs or different kinds of jobs—to go looking for them. De Vido's problem—as any professional who is "typecast"—is that everyone likely to come to him wants what he has already done many times before. That is why, if you (like De Vido) want to diversify your practice, you must reach out to prospects that you have identified. A marketing plan helps you find and contact them.

Photo: Peter Aaron/ESTO

Professional photography is an important marketing tool for De Vido. He uses it for project description sheets as well as for publication of his work. De Vido's townhouse in Brooklyn Heights is shown at the left, while above is the Leader house in Franklin Lakes, New Jersey.

Jeanne Hartnett & Associates, Inc.

43 East Ohio Street, Suite 1022,
Chicago, Illinois 60611

Interior consultants for corporate,
commercial, medical, and
educational design

Established: 1969

Staff (1983): Three principals,
three designers
and liaison architects,
administrative assistant

Educational Background:
Jeanne Hartnett, ASID:
IIT Institute of Design,
Art Institute of Chicago;
Nina Coghlan:
Chicago School of Art and Design:
Philip Deneau:
Harrington Institute of Design

Professional Society.
American Society of Interior Designers

Jeanne Hartnett,
President

Nina Coghlan,
Vice-President

Philip C. Deneau,
Director of Design

PROFESSIONAL FRAMEWORK.
Jeanne Hartnett's firm has attempted to present an image to corporations that jibes with their own self-perceptions. In that sense, her practice is similar to other present-day architectural and design firms that have set up internal hierarchies reflecting corporate organization. Nina Coghlan is Vice President, Philip Deneau is Director of Design, and Henry Kurzynski is Architectural Liaison. Hartnett, whose office is in the heart of Chicago's lively Near North Side, even uses a certain type of business jargon to describe the firm's history and services on the first page of her brochure: "J.H. & Associates provide a comprehensive range of interior planning and design services to corporate, commercial, health care and educational organizations for optimum utilization of human resources, orderly growth and operational efficiencies. Since its inception, the firm has enjoyed continuity of management and expansion, chiefly through client referral and recommendations." She notes that many of her clients "very much appreciate the knowledge that our personnel have been with the firm for a number of years so that continuity is maintained."

GOALS AND OBJECTIVES.
Hartnett's office presents itself, as noted, to prospects in four distinct fields of contract interior design. Thus the primary intention of its marketing program is to secure a larger share of the work available in the Upper Midwest region. Another goal is to expand the marketing area to other areas of the United States, particularly California and parts of the Sunbelt. Furthermore, the firm wished to update its image in a couple of important ways.

MARKETING STRATEGY. First Hartnett wanted to reach out to clients from the office's earlier days to let them know that the practice had matured into one capable of doing major projects in all its specialties. Second, and related to it, the firm decided it was time to lay its old image as a small office aside in favor of one that speaks of "capable professional problem-solvers." Specifically,

they wanted
notion held
that they spe
cally related

PROMOTION
bound brochu
cover letter is
Hartnett and
make their pr
They felt an o
bound booklet
design firms v
peted for jobs,
large architect
themselves tha
designed by Ph
assembled by s
series of existi
nents, looks pr
only $5,000 to
Hartnett says t
what the comp

PROMOTION N
are a number o
ideas in the Ha
are worth shari
choice of comp
needs of the pro
book is being se
consists of abou
project descripti
budgets and dat
followed by the same number of
reprints from relevant publications.
The deep-blue cover is heavy coated
stock and the dropped-out titles in

Hartnett's interiors range from
spaceplanning to space sculpture.
Shown here are offices in Signode
Industries, Inc., in Glenview, Illinois
(left) and the atrium of the East Bank
Club in Chicago (top). Versatility is
stressed in the firm's staff-designed
and assembled brochure (above).

white match the spiral binding. Each
specialty section is introduced by a
line rendering on transparent paper.
One or two four-color photographs of
completed interiors follow them on a
glossy sheet to emphasize the firm's
level of design quality. The typeface
used in the printed portions matches
an IBM Selectric so that "we can mix
proposal data and additional material
to create a complete proposal package." Many of the color shots were
taken by staff photographer Karen
Lindblad and carefully printed so
that light values are similar throughout. Every loose end that might give
away the homemade nature of the
booklet has been resolved so that the
result seems to be a consistent, published product.

EVALUATION. The real marketing
strength of Hartnett's firm lies in its
vigorous program of uncovering and
following up on new business leads.
It is thorough and well-focused without any of the "pushiness" that
designers so often imagine is necessary for successful marketing. Like
other offices that follow up every
possibility, Hartnett sees that task as
a way to learn about the prospect's
needs. It is also, she believes, a way
to share information that will help
the specific client understand what
lies ahead. "Most prospects have not
had past experience," she explains,
"in working with a designer and they
need to understand very clearly what
is involved."

Infield + D'Astolfo, Graphic Design Consultants

49 West 24th Street,
New York City 10010

Graphic design

Established: 1979

Staff (1983): Two principals

Educational Background:
Warren Infield:
Certificate, Cooper Union;
B.S., M.S., Hunter College.
Frank D'Astolfo:
B.S., Pennsylvania State University;
M.F.A. University of Pittsburgh

Teaching Positions:
Warren Infield, Professor of Graphic
Design, Hofstra University
Frank D'Astolfo, Assistant Professor of
Graphic Design, Rutgers
University—Newark

Professional Societies:
American Institute of Graphic Artists
(AIGA)
International Association of Business
Communicators (IABC)

Warren Infield   Frank D'Astolfo

PROFESSIONAL FRAMEWORK.
Infield and D'Astolfo see themselves
as a compact and competitive full-
service graphic design shop whose
strength lies in "the close attention
of both partners to all projects."
Both of them teach graphic design
and that, they claim, gives a vitality
to their practice. They bring to their
own work the same exacting standards that they stress in design
studios at their respective univer-
sities. High-quality work in graphic
design means attention to remark-
ably small details and that takes
time. The primary business problem
that they have, given their enthusiasm for creative work, is estimating
the number of hours that go into a
job, especially since graphic design
services are customarily bid as a
lump sum, part of the delivered project cost to the client.

GOALS AND OBJECTIVES. These
consist of high-quality design, profitability, client service, professional
standing, and diversified practice.
They have avoided specialization.
One characteristic that tends to differentiate graphic design from other
design disciplines is the quick turnover required for most projects. I+D
does some jobs in a few days, completely prepared for the printer; the

average project is handled in three or
four weeks. That creates a nonstop
charrette atmosphere that suits the
two partners who enjoy working
together on weekends and who have
little trouble meeting these deadlines.

MARKETING STRATEGY. Marketing for Infield and D'Astolfo,
therefore, has meant going after
more significant commissions as a
means of gaining more time for
design. Their service-oriented practice produces a very high level of
referrals; and they win a high percentage of the projects they go after.
But they need to do that because
they can afford relatively little time
for marketing under the circumstances. Their evolved marketing
plan depends on extensive analysis of
trade publications in three or four
fields where they look for active
advertiser-prospects whom they then
contact cold. They have also found
that their clients and suppliers, primarily printers, frequently give them
good leads.

PROMOTION TACTICS. Since both
have outgoing personalities, they use
the telephone with great effect for
selling. D'Astolfo is particularly good
at "chatting up" secretaries, who not
only supply lots of inside information

Graphic designers get quick feedback
on the success of their work. Often a
strong piece of design like these by
Infield + D'Astolfo lead to another job
from a user who admired it. Items
shown here are (right) a game designed
for a private organization, (opposite
page, left) cover of the 1983 annual
report for the Educational Testing
Service, (right) merchandising graphics
for a new store at 1205 Lexington
Avenue in Manhattan, and (below)
cover of the 1983 annual report for the
Eastern Paralyzed Veterans Association.

but go out of their way to see that I + D gets a prompt appointment to talk to the boss. One advantage of a small practice is that each completed project can be immediately analyzed for conformity to profitability and design quality goals. As a result, I + D goes after more work in those areas that turn out to be both financially and esthetically profitable. That does not mean they ignore public service work that may pay one-third to one-half of the standard fee.

PROMOTION MATERIALS. As a result of marketing lessons learned, Infield and D'Astolfo have streamlined their own image. They recently dropped the word "Associates" from the firm name in order to emphasize the equal personal involvement of the partners. "Graphic Design Consultants" has been added to better convey the breadth of the firm's services. Because a high proportion of their current work is for corporate clients, a more restrained, dignified graphic expression was created. The preparation of their new brochure serves as an illustration in Part 5 of this book on how to develop high-quality, low-cost promotional material. "Since what we do *is* design, our own literature must express skill at providing exceptional solutions to client communication problems."

EVALUATION. In the early days of their practice, their work included book design for publishers and promotional design for public institutions—approximately one hundred jobs a year. The business appeared to be booming from the start, but after a year or so they realized that overhead was eating up everything that they made: "We were expending tremendous energy and making no money." Although both designers had considerable experience in other cities, they quickly learned that in Manhattan having a lot of projects that met their design quality criteria did not automatically mean that they had a healthy business. Therefore, marketing to Infield + D'Astolfo has meant learning to say "no" to most small jobs and instead identifying and pursuing larger projects that offer both a profit potential and a sense of design satisfaction.

Jaffe Acoustics, Inc.

83 East Avenue,
Norwalk, Connecticut 06851

Acoustical design and consultation
for performing arts facilities

Established: Stagecraft, 1959;
Jaffe Acoustics, Inc. 1968

Staff (1983): Principal, marketing
director, three architectural acoustic
designers, two electro-acoustic designers,
one drafter, four administrators

Educational Background:
Christopher Jaffe:
B.S. (chemical engineering),
Rensselaer Polytechnic Institute (RPI);
Graduate Studies in Theater,
Columbia University;
D.Eng. (Hon.), RPI

Teaching Position: Adjunct Professor, RPI

Professional Societies: Fellow, Acoustical
Society of America (ASA);
Fellow, Audio Engineering Society of
America (AESA);
Fellow, Institute of Acoustics (U.K.);
National Council of Acoustical
Consultants (NCAC);
U.S. Institute of Theater Technology
(USITT)

Christopher Jaffe

New concert halls—(such as the
Merriwether Post Pavilion in Columbia,
Maryland, designed by Frank O. Gehry
& Associates, Inc., Architects (right) and
the Silva Concert Hall in Eugene,
Oregon, designed by Hardy Holzman
Pfeiffer, Architects (page 64)—and
renovated moviehouses—(opposite
page) Majestic Theatre in Dallas, Texas,
designed by John Eberson and restored
by Oglesby Group of Dallas—all benefit
from Jaffe's well-marketed expertise as
an acoustician.

PROFESSIONAL FRAMEWORK.
Christopher Jaffe did not start out to
be an acoustician. In the fifties his
passion was theater. He ran one of
New York City's first Off-Broadway
houses as producer, director, designer, and sometime actor. That aroused
his curiosity about acoustics, and in
1959, Jaffe formed a company that
built acoustical shells for concert
halls throughout North America. He
has gone on to produce a string of
acoustical innovations that have
established him among the leaders of
his profession. His consulting firm is
an innovative small business as well.
Jaffe has developed two electronic
systems that subtly augment the
original sound energy found in performing halls and in corporate
boardrooms. But he is also vigorously seeking to increase his firm's
share of acoustical consulting for
new and renovated performing arts
centers.

GOALS AND OBJECTIVES. In fact,
strengthening his firm's professional
credibility in the performing arts
field has been the principal goal of
his relatively ambitious program of
promotion and sales. Higher fees
from more prestigious jobs has been
his tandem goal with an eye to
increased profitability and controlled
growth of the professional staff. The
creativity of Jaffe's staff is the heart
of what the firm sells. "Our
consultants are not locked into
preconceived ideas," says Jaffe. "We
have developed new tools to meet

acoustic criteria. The state of the art
continues to expand and we are not
afraid to try new methods."

MARKETING STRATEGY. Since
January 1982, Ann Boyar has been
Marketing Director for Jaffe Acoustics. Experienced in public relations
and newsletter production, she has
undertaken a full-scale promoting
and selling effort. As a result of Jaffe's prior work and her campaign,
the firm has experienced rapid
growth to thirteen full-time
employees as of mid-1983. Boyar's
marketing plan of October 1982
takes the national economy strongly
into account, because Jaffe is after a
national market for both his architectural and electro-acoustical
services. Yet the plan remains constant insofar as it aims to meet
prospective clients' needs and keep
on top of promising leads. The actual
strategies change as economic conditions develop and particular job
possibilities appear.

PROMOTION TACTICS. Jaffe Acoustics' leads fall into four categories:
users (symphony managers and
directors); architects who want Jaffe
to be part of their project team;
newspaper articles announcing performing arts center proposals; and
responses to the full-page advertisements Jaffe has run in *Symphony*
magazine. These prospects are then
researched by Boyar to sharpen the
firm's understanding of what the client is hoping to accomplish. As she
learns more about the project, she

sends off still another article or another project description sheet that illuminates an appropriate acoustical issue. Often it takes Boyar six, eight, or even ten contacts with the prospective client before, she says, "They begin to feel they have to respond to all our interest in some way or other."

PROMOTION MATERIAL. In the context of such systematic follow-up is the Jaffe newsletter (shown on page 142). Focusing as they do on high-level, even theoretical acoustic issues, these semi-annual mailers convey the image of immense technical skill. These are coupled with tearsheets of *New York Times* articles reviewing Jaffe's latest concert

hall and reinforced by Boyar's friendly but persistent calls.

EVALUATION. The key is effective follow-up. "It is the hardest thing of all for the small firm which is trying to grow," Boyar says. "You can't make the calls and do the work too. But if you don't keep in touch with your prospects, any money you spend on promotional materials and other efforts to develop the firm's image is just being thrown away. Besides, it is very important to let people know you really want to work for them. A friendly call that also helps them get a better grip on their problem is something that we find is appreciated, not ignored."

Part Three

GETTING STARTED

PLANNING TO MARKET is one thing. Getting started on doing it takes another major act of commitment. There are a number of organizational steps (which precede your first telephone calls and letters) that go beyond planning yet are definitely part of any marketing program. Who is going to be responsible for it overall? Who will be given what specific tasks? How will you make sure the calls and letters get done? Indeed, whom is it you contact once you're ready? Answering all such questions is the purpose of the next three chapters. Even if you have been promoting your services sporadically, take this opportunity to reexamine your efforts and your staff marketing assignments.

It is also the moment to calculate the time and money demands of your new or renewed marketing program. You will see that the nuts and bolts of setting up a promotion and sales campaign are not mysterious in themselves. Each small step of market research and development of solid prospect lists brings you closer to the time when you can confidently reach out to prospects. You will see that there are many ways to go after work. Sources of work will come to mind as you read Chapter 8 that you may never have recognized before. Referrals from former clients, for instance, are one area where you can quite easily increase your new business. Finally, in Chapter 9, the classic dilemma of the very small design office is examined: How do you go out looking for new work when you're busy doing what you already have?

Chapter Seven
ORGANIZING TO MARKET

WHETHER OR NOT you have a fully prepared marketing plan, you must at some point consider how much time and money you can invest in marketing. For the small firm, time will be the prime consideration, if only because there isn't enough money available to worry about spending! Yet that may be an opportunity in disguise. The advantage of a design office over most businesses is that the talents (especially visual skills) for reaching out to find new work are probably already at hand. What is more important even than skills is the enthusiasm and loyalty that can be drawn upon from the staff. Even part-time and student workers are likely to respond with vigor if they understand that marketing success for the office can lead to a more stable practice. Use those energies well (because they're already on the payroll) before you consider hiring experts to do your marketing.

BUDGETING TIME AND MONEY

A FEW HOURS each week consistently set aside for finding new sources of work is better than a much more ambitious program that loses steam before the results begin to show. Marketing is a very long race and the first couple of years are definitely uphill. The biggest morale problem is that nothing much will happen that can be attributed to marketing for the first six months, and people will get discouraged. They must be helped to understand that, just as the design process can seem a long and arbitrary ordeal to clients—maybe even as a "waste of time"—so to designers unfamiliar with marketing strategies and rhythms, the temptation will be to give up too soon. Although it varies from one design discipline to another, between one and three years must pass before the plan will begin to pay off.

The participants in this book report a consistent 10 to 12 percent of gross annual billings devoted to promoting and selling design services (see box on page 67). In the past, conventional wisdom has indicated that 7 percent was adequate for marketing in our field. A survey of architectural firms, including many large ones, by the Society for Marketing Professional Services (SMPS, 1982) showed that 6.3 percent of annual income went to marketing; 71 percent of that was for salaries; the balance for out-of-pocket expenses. It appears that design firms having less than a dozen employees, with correspondingly lower dollar income than most of the firms in the SMPS survey, must expect to

---

Amount of Time Spent on Marketing (as Reported)

Judith Chafee:
"Ten solid hours a week."

Will Ching:
Part-time marketing administrator spends fifteen hours a week.

Jeanne Hartnett:
She spends thirty hours per week; her two associates put in twenty and ten hours per week, respectively.

Infield + D'Astolfo:
The two partners spend 10 percent of their time.

Jaffe Acoustics:
Ann Boyar is full-time director of marketing.

Jordan/Mitchell:
The partners aim for twelve hours per week each (but often fail to meet that goal).

Gere Kavanaugh:
She spends one morning per week.

Koster and Holzheimer:
Bill Koster devotes 56 percent of his time, plus a full-time marketing coordinator.

Gordon Perry:
Twenty-five percent of his time.

Radford-Biddison:
Pam Radford spends 25 percent of her time; Gail Biddison puts in somewhat less time.

Voorsanger and Mills:
Each partner spends five to fifteen hours per week.

The others report five hours or less per week.

devote a significantly larger chunk of what they earn in the next few years to marketing. That is the result of increased competition for the most part. More elaborate promotional materials than were customary in the past, however, also account for the additional expense, as do higher salaries, higher travel costs, higher costs of entertaining.

The largest component of any marketing program is salaries. Those of the sixteen designers who supplied information on their categories of cost indicated that principal and staff salaries ranged from 60 to 80 percent of their total promotion and sales expense. Even though salaries are a somewhat "soft" expense, because in most cases they would be paid anyway, the money for promotional materials, travel and entertainment must come out of your firm's annual budget. It is hardly sensible for a small design firm to borrow money in order to promote itself more aggressively. There are two reasons: the cost of interest is perhaps more than the profit it will generate; since marketing is a long-term process, the debt must be paid off slowly, thus raising the cost even more. Therefore the extent of your marketing program will largely be determined by how much current income you can afford to spend on it (see example in the accompanying box).

It means that most design firms must move into marketing gradually. Again that may not be a bad idea. It is much wiser to build your program on what you already know or what you have accomplished than to take big chances with elaborate promotional materials or an expensive marketing consultant.

ASSIGNING RESPONSIBILITIES

U SE YOUR FIRM'S TIME efficiently by assigning responsibilities to everyone involved in the marketing program. Then set up a definite hour each week when they report. As Ray Gindroz of UDA states, "We are finding that the most important part of the process is the rigorous scheduling of meetings in which we review the list of marketing possibilities. 'Out of sight, out of mind' applies in two ways: If we don't see the list of potential clients, we tend to forget to keep in touch with them. And if we don't keep in touch with our potential clients, they soon forget about us."

It is almost certain that less effort than is promised will actually be made; that is why frequent, blame-free reporting sessions are necessary. Those who are not making much progress can be gently pumped up and the ones who are can be rewarded with attention and a chance to tell about what seems to be working for them.

There must be a head cheerleader: someone in the firm who is in charge of the meetings and who makes clear each time how important the marketing work is. If the meetings do not have top priority, soon the best-designed marketing plan will drift into the background. For many firms the person in charge of marketing will be obvious: the "founder" or senior partner who has always brought in work or who has the connections that have worked in the past. But if there is not a clear choice, then it should be the principal who has been the most enthusiastic proponent of having a marketing plan at all. It should be someone with an "overview" perspective rather than a technically oriented point of view—someone at ease with people on the telephone and in meetings. He or she must help everyone else get past the psychological barrier of reaching out. Most designers hate to have to "make a sale." It is especially difficult when most of the contacts will be negative or generally fruitless to begin with.

Once selected, the person in charge of marketing must devote as

Percentage of Gross Annual Income Spent on Marketing (as reported)

AKA:
Ten percent

Judith Chafee:
Ten percent
(not including principal's salary)

Jeanne Hartnett:
Three percent
(not including salaries)

Infield + D'Astolfo:
Approximately ten percent

Jaffe Acoustics:
Ten to twelve percent

Jordan/Mitchell:
Twelve and a half percent

Koster and Holzheimer:
About twelve percent

Gordon Perry:
Ten to fifteen percent

Radford-Biddison:
Ten to fifteen percent

Voorsanger and Mills:
Five percent (not including principals' time)

The others did not report a figure.

much time as possible (25 percent is clearly the minimum and 50 percent or more desirable) on all its aspects: promoting, selling, organizing, planning, scheduling, and constantly reassessing goals and strategies.

Everyone who shares in the profits of the firm should be involved in marketing. Not just principals but every staff member who can be enlisted to work on the program should do it. The dynamics of a marketing program are so fragile for the first year, let alone for the ongoing effort, that they need everyone's support.

"Support" is a word with another meaning in this case. Marketing support means the continuing staff work that must accompany the prospecting efforts of the principals. Translate your plan into fixed quantities of action required each week. Who is going to do what tasks? And how will the principals' work be coordinated with the support effort on a daily basis? Marketing support includes: response to referrals and requests for information about the firm; sending out "packages"—tearsheets, brochures, project descriptions, resumes, and so on; writing prospecting letters; arranging meetings; making cold telephone calls; making follow-up calls; getting information from newspapers and other sources; designing and producing mailings; preparing presentations; and of course keeping track of what the partners are supposed to be doing. The overall amount of activity is determined by the marketing plan.

As for individual quotas, the partner-in-charge must be especially sensitive to how much each person can actually accomplish. The number of activities assigned should be large enough so that a certain period of time is worth putting aside to do them. Too many, on the other hand, can mean that nothing at all will be done.

STAFFING OPTIONS

THERE ARE THREE distinct ways to provide for marketing support: using present staff, taking on a part-time consultant, and recruiting a full-time marketing specialist. While such decisions should be an integral part of the marketing plan, the mechanics and financial consequences deserve close study because the choice largely determines, in practical terms, how much marketing you are actually going to do. One- or two-partner firms are likely to find the first option the only one they can exercise at present. Three-or-more-partner firms, on the other hand, can probably choose whichever option seems likely to produce the best results for the money spent.

If you make use of your present staff there are two options: to appoint a secretary or a junior staffer. Bill Koster has promoted his long-time secretary-receptionist to Marketing Coordinator. Others have enlisted an apprentice or junior professional colleague who is interested in marketing. Both of these types of people will need considerable guidance from the principal in charge of marketing. It is crucial that the principal's vision of how the marketing plan is to be implemented be kept clearly in mind by all parties. Just as in the development of a design proposal, the original concept must not get lost in the daily pressure of details and compromises.

The second possibility is the part-time consultant. Marketing professionals with considerable skill and training, thanks to the growing numbers of business school graduates in the United States, are readily available to design firms. There are consultants and firms that serve only designers and architects (listed on page 43). These people can quickly and efficiently focus on your marketing problems and provide

> ### *Example of How to Compute a Marketing Budget*
>
> A useful way to uncover how much money you have available to spend is to take your gross billings for the past year (or better still, your estimated billings for the current year). Allocate, say, 8 percent of it to marketing (if you have kept records for recent years, substitute your own figure).
> Assume you have gross annual billings of $200,000. Eight percent is $16,000. Typically, you would allocate 75 to 80 percent (or $12,800) to travel, entertainment, lead-finding, and other direct selling costs, and $3,200 for such promotional costs as photography, newsletters and press releases, award program entry fees, and so on.
> And remember that you must include in these figures prorated salary dollars for personnel time spent on marketing as shown in the table on page 69.

Comparative Costs:
Three Marketing Program Budgets

$15,000 per year for marketing

Salaries:	Principal	250 hr/yr × $25.00/hr =	$6,250
	Secretary	750 hr/yr × $7.50/hr =	5,625

Out-of-pocket expenses including promotion (costs spread over two years)	=	3,125
Total		$15,000

$40,000 per year for marketing

Salaries:	Principals	350 hr/yr × $35.00/hr =	$12,250
	Marketing Coordinator	2,000 hr/yr × $9.00/hr =	18,000

Out-of-pocket expenses including promotion	=	9,750
Total		$40,000

$75,000 per year for marketing

Salaries:	Principals	500 hr/yr × $50.00/hr =	$25,000
	Marketing Director	2,000 hr/yr × $12.50/hr =	25,000
	Secretary	750 hr/yr × $7.50/hr =	5,625

Out-of-pocket expenses including promotion	=	19,375
Total		$75,000

Note: Salaries represent from 74 to 80% of the total budget.

Salaries represent from 74 to 80 percent of the total budget for these examples. Although marketing effort is charged to overhead, it is important to keep records of time spent doing it. Level of effort depends on such factors as ratio of referral work, local versus national effort, number of design specialties, and attitude of principals to marketing.

useful advice. Typically, the consultant will work with you for two or three days, charging $600 to $1,200 per day. You then have the option to reorganize the office as recommended, to make partial changes, or to continue as before. Consultants are also available for periodic evaluation of your marketing program as you pursue it. They offer the benefit of business experience focused on our field without the continuing expense of a staff specialist.

The third major approach is to take on a full-time marketing specialist as Jaffe Acoustics did when Ann Boyar was hired early in 1982. As Marketing Director, Boyar is responsible for the firm's marketing program. Even so, she is technically still limited to offering suggestions to Jaffe and must wait for his approval before she can act. The program as a whole costs a hefty $75,000 a year and has contributed to a rapid increase in Jaffe's workload and prestige among acoustical consultants. The question of whether you need such a specialist is probably answered by the price tag. A smaller firm, unless there is enough money already in the bank to finance it, could experience severe cash flow problems while waiting for such a marketing program to pay off.

Finally, no matter what staffing arrangement you choose or what scope of program, as principal you must be committed to active, daily participation. Otherwise it will either die of inactivity or, if your marketer is determined to succeed, may go off in a direction that you neither anticipated nor wanted.

UNCOVERING LEADS

ATHOROUGH marketing plan identifies the kinds of information you need to push the program forward. While leads for jobs frequently come in from people with whom you have close contact, it is also possible to find prospects by carefully reading newpapers, magazines, and various commercial information sources. "I read the paper with scissors," says interiors and furniture designer Gere Kavanaugh.

Another useful source of prospects for a design firm is the relatively new breed of "city" magazines. They are usually fat with ads placed by businesses which are after that same affluent audience you are. There is no reason why you can't go after the advertisers as well as the readers.

A periodical source that designers often overlook (for both prospects and publication of completed projects) is the hundreds of business publications serving specific businesses and industries. These can be located through press directories such as *Bacon's Publicity Checker.* This and similar directories are probably available in your local public library. Businesses commonly organize trade associations which publish membership lists that often include information on the annual sales and size of manufacturing facilities of each member.

In addition to an enormous range of printed information on marketing sources, personal and social contacts can yield valuable leads as well. When you have decided to market in a new city or region, look up acquaintances with business connections in the area and take them to lunch. Also consider joining the Chamber of Commerce in your city—if you didn't do it years ago—and when you want to expand into another community, you'll be welcomed at the local chamber luncheons as a colleague, not a stranger.

Every design field has a related commercial structure populated by suppliers, contractors, and manufacturers' representatives, many of whom like nothing better than an opportunity to gossip about what's going on in your business world. Not only can you get, for the trouble of accepting a lunch invitation, the real truth about how busy your competitors are, but you can learn about potential business developments long before they appear in the press. The additional advantage in this case is that you can probably then call the right person at the subject company directly with your informant as a reference. Nine times out of ten, you'll get an appointment for the asking.

IDENTIFYING THE BEST PROSPECTS

THE DESIGNER'S ultimate goal in winnowing the vast amounts of commercial information available today is to find a dozen or two clients each year who will offer stimulating project opportunities and pay their bills on time. The challenge, of course, is to sift through the news and the rumors to seek out, not just everyone who needs your skills, but the individuals with whom you can work productively. As you go after new business, you are looking for jobs you want and, at the same time, jobs you have a realistic chance to win.

What to Look for in the Newspaper

Potential real estate projects, including renovations

Individuals or firms proposing or doing projects related to your marketing program

Towns and counties planning and passing bond issues

Legal advertisements (requests for proposals by governmental agencies)

Planning proposals that could mean future work

Announcements of new businesses: retail, corporate, real estate, and so on

New business ventures by established firms

Executive promotions and retirements

Economic trends in your city or region

Service organization news

Advertisements for services or products related to your interests

When designers suddenly find themselves with several potential jobs, they often panic and say to themselves, "What if they all say yes? How will we ever get the work done?" Here's where you can make a big mistake: Don't start worrying about getting a project done until you have a signed contract and a retainer that has cleared the bank. Many not only start planning for this new workload too soon, but go around telling everyone about the "new project." Sometimes these anticipated commissions do work out of course, but too many times, something goes wrong. Try to maintain a sensible perspective about the uncertainties of getting new jobs.

A useful system for devising priorities for pursuing leads can be found in Appendix B: Checklist for Go/No-Go Decisions. This process is especially important at those times when several prospects have appeared at once and you must determine how much time and effort to put into each. When you have decided which of them suit you best, you can focus energy, as well as calls and letters, where it counts. Check them out using your business network: Call former clients and acquaintances who may know the individuals involved; call suppliers and bankers who can give you financial information. Don't be timid about checking out prospects' credit ratings and, if possible, their ability to pay for the specific project they propose. If you hear that another designer may have been involved in this project or may have worked for this client in the past, be smart and call him or her to learn why the relationship has ended. You may be glad you did.

Sources of Project Information

Dodge Construction News: Chicago, $130 annual subscription; Denver, San Francisco, Los Angeles

Dodge Reports: $1,400 and up annual subscription; architects should keep in touch with appropriate architectural reporter, McGraw-Hill Information Systems Co.

Commerce Business Daily, U.S. Department of Commerce: $175 annual subscription (first-class mailing) or $100 (second-class mailing), Superintendent of Documents, Government Printing Office, Washington, D.C. 20402

Herb Ireland's "Sales Prospector": $98 annual subscription for one edition, $695 for all fifteen; monthly newsletter published in fourteen U.S. and one Canadian editions; 751 Main Street, P.O. Box 518, Waltham, MA 02254

Medical Project Report: monthly project listings published in five U.S. regional editions, $175 annual subscription for one edition, $675 for all five; James & Douglas Publishers, Inc., P.O. Box 7375, Marietta, GA 30065

Commercial clipping services: offering national and/or regional coverage; typical prices $50 per month plus $.75 per clipping or $1,100 per year (includes 1,000 clippings)

Criteria for Analyzing Prospects

Does the job conform to your marketing plan?

How far is the jobsite from your office?

Is it worth the travel time (even if you get paid)?

Do you have other work in progress nearby?

Are there other possibilities with the same client or in the same area?

How does the project relate to other things you've done?

Does it pose any unusual site or design problems?

Is the budget and time schedule adequate to a good design job?

Can you make a profit on the fee proposed for this project?

Is the scope of the job appropriate to your present staff?

If it's too big, can you find good people fast enough to get it done on time?

Is the client organization responsive to your ideas?

Will you have to "educate" them to sell your design concepts?

Do you feel comfortable with the prospect?

How badly does this group need professional design help?

Is this a commission you have a good chance to win?

Would you do this job if you had enough other work?

COMMERCIAL
MAILING LISTS

Y OU MAY HAVE wondered about buying or renting mailing lists of prospects for a direct mail program consisting of your brochure, your newsletter, or some other form of message. Most companies (see yellow pages) rent lists which focus on specific categories so that you pay for a higher proportion of likely candidates. They usually offer free catalogs of the available lists. A selection of 1,000 bank executives in the New York City metropolitan area, for instance, costs about $75 for one-time use. Purchase of a list is about twice the cost of rental.

One strategy that might make such lists worthwhile for you is to purchase a rather specific geographic list (you can select the information zip code by zip code) in one of the specialties you are marketing and then use it three ways: First send a specially prepared folder with a cover letter to all the names; then as time permits, follow up with cold calls that will be slightly warmer than usual because of the earlier mailing, gradually reducing the original set of names to a good short list (including updated and corrected names and titles); finally a more personalized mailing with brochures or portfolios could follow later. The entire process might take six months but would represent a well-integrated contact program.

Many of the companies that sell mailing lists also offer complete direct mail service (typesetting, printing, stuffing, as well as posting). The Cheshire method—automatic machines that print and affix gummed labels directly to envelopes—is the main technique used today for volume mailing. Prices vary across the country, but in New York City, a thousand preprinted gummed labels put on standard business envelopes, stuffed with one sheet folded by the mailer, and mailed first class costs about $95, not including any of the materials or postage. The best practice for personalized letters, however, is to type the envelope address and use a stamp rather than a postage meter.

MONITORING YOUR
MARKETING EFFORTS

N O MARKETING PROGRAM can be effective without careful means of keeping track of the results. Progress must be charted so that people can be encouraged and rewarded as they do the work. Monthly statistics don't take a lot of time to compile (see corresponding chart) and, when graphed over a year or two, help visually oriented designers stay more interested in how things are going. This analysis can help you spot the marketing "failures"—the techniques that aren't working—so that your energies can be redirected.

The best way to keep track of individual prospects is 5 × 8 cards. They allow total flexibility of arrangement and are easy to revise, update, and weed out. Tickler tabs can be affixed to the most promising leads, and 500 or 1,000 cards take up very little space. The microcomputer is also an excellent means of keeping prospecting information in order and at hand. See Appendix A for marketing with microcomputers.

MHD

1984 MARKETING PROGRESS REPORTS
MICKEY, HICKEY + DICKEY · INDUSTRIAL DESIGNERS

ASSIGNMENTS FOR REPORTING SESSION:

1984 TO 1984

1984

MARKETER:

NO.	DISPOSITION

MARKET
- COLD TELEPHONE CALLS
- GENERAL LETTERS
- PERSONAL LETTERS
- BROCHURE/COVER LETTERS
- FOLLOW-UP LETTERS
- CANVASSING VISITS
- INTERVIEWS
- OTHER PROGRESS

MARKET
- COLD TELEPHONE CALLS
- GENERAL LETTERS
- PERSONAL LETTERS
- BROCHURE/COVER LETTERS
- FOLLOW-UP LETTERS
- CANVASSING VISITS
- INTERVIEWS
- OTHER PROGRESS

MARKET
- COLD TELEPHONE CALLS
- GENERAL LETTERS
- PERSONAL LETTERS
- BROCHURE/COVER LETTERS
- FOLLOW-UP LETTERS
- CANVASSING VISITS
- INTERVIEWS
- OTHER PROGRESS

Not every firm needs as complete a progress form as this. But the advantage of a standard format is revealed later when an entire year's work can be easily measured by scanning a dozen such sheets.

Chapter Eight
SEEKING OPPORTUNITIES

Opportunities for work run the gamut from referrals—where it seeks you out—to entrepreneurial projects—where you seek it out, indeed, you create it. Marketing, therefore, is making the best use of whatever comes along rather than just waiting for the next job to appear on your plate.

As Gail Biddison says: "Our first contact with potential clients may be in professional, social or even casual encounters. We market literally all the time. A recent reference and interview for a major corporate job came through a saleswoman in a dress shop whose husband was project manager for the corporation."

According to Ken Arutunian: "The practice was started in 1968 and for ten years relied mostly on referrals. There was no need to develop a marketing program. We were even able to expand the scope of activities in the office primarily by referrals and also by keeping our eyes and ears open to new things going on around us."

MAKING THE MOST OF REFERRALS

To begin, the question is not just "referrals" but how to maximize the number of project possibilities that come out of situations where people who know you and your work influence others who need design services.

The thing to keep in mind is that those whom you have served diligently and well are almost always concerned and solicitous about your business future. That is why, once you have completed your first designer job successfully, you have the beginnings of a marketing organization in place.

Let's begin with former clients then. They are the primary source of work for most designers. Do you let them know how important they are to you? Every six months, De Vido puts together a package of material on recently completed jobs and sends it to all his old clients.

In business it is very common for people working together to speculate on possible ways that they can make future deals. Designers rarely do that. We seem to prefer keeping our hands clean and our cupboards bare. There probably is more opportunity for "repeat business" with former clients than you've ever dreamed of. Pamela Waters is one designer who doesn't let that opportunity pass. When she reads an article about a client she hasn't worked for in a year or two, she says, "I send him a note congratulating him. He calls me up and says, 'Nice to hear from you. How come you're not doing any work for us?'"

Current clients have even more potential to assist your marketing aims. Because your project is occupying a lot of their daily life as well as yours, they think of you often. At the same time, they are more interested in being nice to you (in order to get your best efforts) than they will be when the job is finished. All you have to do is ask them, in a nice way, to keep an eye out for people they know who might be "in the market" for design services like yours.

Keep in mind that when anyone recommends you, they are—in a social sense—going out on a limb. That is why every referral must be given full attention. Not only should you be careful to acknowledge the recommendation with thanks, but if you should decide to refuse the project for any reason, you must call the person who sent the prospect to you before you actually turn it down.

Socializing, a form of marketing that is reputedly the way "certain designers" get all their work, is a process that each individual practitioner must work out. Everyone understands that almost any human contact we have may lead to a professional relationship. But some of us can act on that knowledge more effectively than others.

If you are deciding that you must promote more effectively to achieve professional goals, then pay some attention to your manner and appearance. One easy source of help is to look at the people to whom you wish to sell your services. Study their style and try to match it. The more you resemble them, the more comfortable they will be.

Another means of developing your social skills is to ask a salesperson for one of your suppliers to help you. Selling ability can be acquired through study and practice. Keep in mind that people are generally fascinated by designers. There aren't that many of us that you run the risk of boring those with whom you discuss your design philosophy or vision.

GOING AFTER SPECIFIC MARKETS

DESIGNERS, especially architects, love to think of themselves as able to apply the "design process" to any problem. Yet the client, in most cases, is not looking for the "fresh approach" such a generalist brings, but the assurance that the designer can handle all the technicalities that the problem presents. The question is: Can you compete successfully for work in a field about which you know little?

If you choose to try, the first step is to assimilate the knowledge—including the jargon—of the field you are competing in. By reading intensively, consulting "experts," and mastering the economics of the project beforehand, you could well, given your basic skills as a designer in your field, appear to be a viable candidate among specialists. Then your presentation must be rich with evidence that you know as much about the problem as any expert. Furthermore you will have to prove to the client that you can save him or her money and time through your "fresh approach." It is a high-risk approach to design marketing because it takes so much energy to prepare yourself. On the other hand, that you cared enough to immerse yourself in learning the prospects' needs may mean more to them than the expertise offered by specialists.

However disagreeable you may find it as a designer, the fact is that specialization is the only *logical* way to market your services. Our corporate society is built upon specialization, and the great majority of potential design clients seek the quietly competent response to their

New market information can be found in four types of places: reference books and magazines, experts and conferences. If you have specific prospects in a new market, ask to visit their factories or jobsites: Learn about the process from managers and technicians, especially about the shortcuts and cost saving ideas that work. Such people often gladly share with anyone truly interested in their work.

Reference Materials:
Textbooks

Training manuals

Industry handbooks

Manufacturing process descriptions

Materials information sources

Economic statistics

Business Magazines:
Overview articles

Economic forecasts and business projections

Simplified manufacturing process articles

Names of prominent individuals and organizations

Advertisements offering further information

Experts:
Consulting engineers and other technical sources

Salespeople, distributors, and retailers

Conferences:
Marketing conferences and seminars

Conventions and tradeshows

needs—reasonably attractive, finished on time, and within the budget. Who knows best how to do that? The firm with the track record and the client references. "Specialization is the *only* way you can deliver quality service to your clients," says Bill Koster. "Fees do not support quality 'Jack-of-all-trades' practices so you must be firm in your commitment to expertise in just a few project types and give your marketing plan time to work for you."

Far from being a boring, repetitious process, specialization can be continuing education of the most fascinating sort for a designer. In order for your work to capture the attention of potential clients in whatever field you are focusing on, it must convey an authoritative grasp of the issues that interest them. Everyone tries to prove that they can get the job done on time and within their clients' budget. A typical designer selection committee looks for something more: the ability to provide the optimal solution to their particular problem.

The interview is where publication in the magazines that *they* read helps as well. Projects shown there can be valuable indeed, such as an article on patients' room design in a journal for hospital administrators or examples of corporate identity designs and logos in a business magazine for corporate executives.

Equally important, of course, is to keep abreast of company politics—changes and trends, shifts of key executive personnel within your specialties and marketing area. It is always frustrating to have to go to corporate or institutional headquarters and reintroduce yourself—"reselling yourself" in fact—to the latest vice-president in charge of retaining designers even though you've done work for them many times before. But that is a requirement of consistent follow-up.

Think of your body of clients and prospects as a small community of which you are an active member, your professional network. By marketing vigorously, you can also help them make business connections with each other. That way, the people in the speciality you are pursuing begin to hear your name from others whom they trust. The best thing of all is when they begin to "talk about you behind your back." In short, marketing can help increase your referrals at the same time that it identifies new opportunities for you.

The process of developing and cultivating a constantly growing circle of friends and business associates has come to be called "networking," and it often can be the most direct and productive source of new and continuing work. It calls for a ruthlessly updated address and phone file, and a process of keeping your network apprised of what you are doing.

MARKETING TO OTHER DESIGNERS

ANOTHER SMALL community to which you may wish to market is the design field itself. For some of the participants in this book, other designers are a very important source of business: architects frequently hire interior designers, graphic designers, landscape architects, acousticians, and the various engineering design disciplines, for example. However, it can be a tougher market than the broader business world. Many times professional relationships, such as that between an architect and a graphic designer, are permanent and there is little likelihood that, no matter how attractive your approach, the old collaborator will be put aside.

Nonetheless there are definite marketing strategies that can gradually build your reputation among other design professionals. The newsletter distributed by Jaffe Acoustics is a good case in point. Each issue features a technical development by Jaffe and explains it in very straightforward language while sandwiching in dignified mention of all the concert halls the firm has worked on recently. You learn something from it and you feel that Jaffe's is certainly an impressive outfit.

Master the needs of these potential designer-clients. A common complaint by architects and interior designers about mechanical engineers, for instance, is that they don't have a "design sense." They put their grilles and vents in places that ruin the building's appearance. Mechanical engineers who expressed any esthetic interest in their marketing materials would have a big leg-up finding clients. Read the trade magazines of the group you want to work for—you'll quickly find out what matters to them. Once you have gotten a grip on those issues, seek opportunities to speak at their professional meetings, regional conferences, and the appropriate design schools. Use the time as a chance to talk about how similar your design approach is to theirs and how the two can work together better in the future.

Ken Arutunian, as head of a landscape architecture firm, finds that much of his work comes from architects, planners, and A/E firms that are the prime consultants on the job. Therefore, his marketing consists of focusing on a specific project. Lots of time and money go into preparing proposals for interviews where several competitors may make presentations. That has meant that AKA, which develops all its promotional material in-house, has had to continually adapt its proposals.

RESPONDING TO GOVERNMENT RFPs

ARUTUNIAN has this to say when dealing with Requests for Proposals (RFPs) from government agencies: "We have had very good success responding to RFPs for park and recreation work from city and county governmental bodies, often making the shortlist. Our record of actually being selected for the job is maybe one in six to eight shortlists. The problem is that at the interview level, you are competing with the top level of the profession in the region. In these competitive times, firms much larger and more prestigious than ours are competing for relatively modest jobs."

The time-consuming aspect of government RFP work is the SF 254/255 forms. Standard Form 254: Architect-Engineer and Related Services Questionnaire is a general description of the firm, and Standard Form 255 (which has the same title) is a specific description for the project under consideration. These forms are set up for the interviewers at the agency to determine that your firm has been around long enough and has sufficient forces—by their standards—to do the job. A prearranged set of associates is the way most designers attempt to meet that challenge. A good deal of time can go into assembling such a group and agreeing on the business aspects. "Our few experiences in preparing applications for small government and school jobs requiring 254 and 255 forms," says Judith Chafee, "have been very expensive and disappointing. We are now engaged in some 'backdoor' efforts—small, unglamorous school jobs—that are establishing a working relationship with officialdom. This is a much better investment."

Sometimes getting a government job, for the small firm, is far worse than not being selected. The demand for thorough bidding documents, including fat specification books, means that a larger than usual part of the fee may go for production. You must also consider the possibility of late payments and arrange your financial planning accordingly. Since the 70s, some financial officers try to make what they have go further by delaying payments. That can be disastrous for a design business with inadequate financing.

All these problems make it seem that official jobs are best left to the larger, better-organized firms. Yet in smaller towns and rural counties, much of the bureaucratic complication that is found in large cities or in federal projects is avoided. Not all public projects require the federal 254/255 forms. And in areas where little commercial development is underway, government commissions can be attractive.

Those of you who choose to go after government work using the SF 254 and 255 route can write for an excellent compendium of lucid articles on the subject, *Preparing Effective Proposals,* published by Michael Hough, *Professional Services Management Journal,* Box 11316, Newington, Conn. 06111. There is a modest charge.

CREATING MARKETS

STILL ANOTHER source of work is the creation of your own markets. However, entrepreneurial ventures can be risky for the small design firm. It is wise to undertake them only with time and money that can be lost without consequence. As long as you never forget that you are gambling, speculative projects can be wonderful fun.

Two clearly different project scales are available for designers: product development and real estate development. As an industrial designer, Gordon Perry has created designs for manufacturers that range from pasta machines to office furniture and exercise equipment, all on a royalty basis. Although he sometimes receives a modest payment for his costs as he develops the design, Perry's primary source of income will be approximately 5 percent of whatever income the manufacturer receives.

In the American free-market economy, real estate development is the way that most housing and commercial building gets done. It offers architects as well as interior and graphic designers a chance to get involved in larger and more interesting projects than may otherwise be available. But the risk is greater too. The developer is paid a minimal fee when the work is done, sometimes with a promise of more money or a share in profits later if all goes well. A designer must build for profit, which means that elegant design and detail seldom survive except in "luxury" buildings. The exposure offered by such projects is valuable only if the designer promotes it vigorously to other prospects. UDA Architects sometimes seeks projects jointly with developers. They find that this collaboration introduces urban design action at an early stage, creating a climate of achievement for citizens and government agencies alike.

MARKETING THROUGH PUBLIC
AWARENESS: LECTURING

"SPREADING YOUR name around" is, to many designers, one of the most attractive forms of marketing. Three principal areas of activity are lecturing, public service, and professional society work.

GENERAL AUDIENCES. Lecturing can be painful for some designers—requiring long preparation laced with anxiety—but it is a skill worth mastering. If you are an actor manqué, on the other hand, you will have no trouble responding to every opportunity that comes your way. These lectures offer the beguiling possibility that afterwards someone will come forward and say, "I loved what you said about restaurants. When can we get together to talk about working together on one that I'm planning to open soon?"

The important thing about successful public speaking is to keep the audience's interests uppermost in your mind. Do not look at it simply as an opportunity to run through your usual slide show. If the banker's wife who is in the audience decides you are a self-centered windbag, the banker may be influenced, but not the way you want.

Don't take on speaking engagements half-heartedly. Preparation doesn't need to take hours, but be sure that you discuss the topic with the person who asks you to talk. Find out who will be coming to hear you and what things they may want to know. Then be sure you follow the advice. One good idea, if you must use slides to talk about design, is to include the work of some other firms and to say nice things about them.

Lecturing Guidelines

1. Research
a. How big will the audience be?

b. Who are they?

c. What are they interested in?

d. How much time will you have?

e. What kind of room?

f. Will there be amplification?

2. Writing
a. Shape your material to suit what you've learned about the audience.

b. Limit your scope to one major idea or concept with no more than three subheadings.

c. Use examples and illustrations frequently; humor never hurts.

d. Employ short sentences rather than compound construction.

e. Keep the talk short so that there will be time for questions.

f. Outline the completed speech on one piece of paper rather than reading it verbatim or putting it on cards.

g. Rehearse what you're going to say with someone ahead of time.

3. Slides
a. Call ahead and make sure the equipment will be there and in good order; better still, bring your own.

b. Arrive half an hour early to set up the projector.

c. Avoid using your standard interview-and-prospect slideshow.

d. Assume one slide per minute as a rough calculation of time (don't bring a lot more slides figuring you can rush through them—edit beforehand!).

e. If slides are the heart of your lecture, you may want to let them trigger your thoughts rather than write out a script—this can be tricky if you get too involved in each slide.

4. Presentation
a. If it does not make you uncomfortable, allow the audience to ask questions while you are speaking.

b. If they are whispering or otherwise restless, try talking very softly or stop altogether until you have their full attention.

c. Speak as slowly and clearly as you can; put notes on your script to remind you to go slowly.

d. Move your gaze across the audience and find individuals upon whom you can focus for a few sentences before moving on.

SPECIALIZED AUDIENCES. When prospects for your design services gather to hear you speak, you have an opportunity for long-range promotion. The marketing message should be subordinated to one that emphasizes the audience's aspirations. When Ralph Appelbaum, for instance, addresses a meeting of museum curators, he talks about raising the standards of their field through good design, not about how he can do the best job for them. You know what client-groups in your field hope to accomplish. Let them know you share their goals. Each auditor will form an impression of you as a professional even if you don't show them your work as well.

STUDENT AUDIENCES. Designers often see lecturing at professional and art schools as a way of attracting young talent to their offices. (Developing an outstanding staff directly affects marketing potential.) It may be a great ego-puffing event, but even so the wise designer knows to avoid the "here-is-my-latest-work" format. Put yourself in their shoes—what would you as a student want to learn from a mature practitioner? That is largely why Will Ching (who often represents the Institute of Business Designers to student groups) addresses their concerns about the future from a broad, professionwide perspective. The best students come forward at the end to express their interest even though he said nothing about his own practice.

PUBLIC SERVICE

GERE KAVANAUGH feels strongly that professionals ought to participate as citizens in local government: "I think that the design community—architects, interior designers, and graphic designers—should be more involved in civic affairs. If you make money in a place, it makes sense to plow some time back in to create a better climate for yourself and your business."

Actually, most designers are rather apolitical, eschewing the public spotlight for fear of offending a potential client. But productive public service does not necessarily involve controversy and headlines. One important consequence of long-term service, such as on a zoning board or the kind of public review committees that mayors like to set up when they don't want to make any mistakes, is that you meet the city's decision-makers in an informal yet focused framework.

Such contacts lead to networking on a far more effective level than when you present yourself to these same individuals as just another architect or designer looking for work. When you call such people later to propose a lunch, chances are that your invitation will be enthusiastically accepted. Your guest will no doubt want to know more about your work.

A press notice for something other than your business can be excellent publicity. That is, after all, one of the primary reasons why individuals need public relations. The intent of gaining public confidence through community service, as it relates to marketing design services, is to bring your firm's name to people's attention. Thus, when you enter the interview room, there will be a sense of positive identification in the minds of the committee, not just a good-natured blank.

PROFESSIONAL SOCIETIES

WILL CHING says, "Belong and become active in your professional organization. Clients understand it as a stable dedication to your profession, particularly if there is licensing involved. If you become an officer, let your peers and clients know through press releases." Ching sent one out, for instance, when he was appointed to the National Council for Interior Design Qualification.

Gordon Perry, Treasurer of the New York Chapter of the Industrial Design Society of America, notes "some fascinating discussions with colleagues in this business because there are few people who understand the frustrations and problems that a private practitioner has as they do."

There are tangible marketing benefits to be gained from professional society work (see accompanying box). Voorsanger and Mills actually got a commission out of their work. In 1981 they were selected by their colleagues at the New York Chapter of the American Institute of Architects to redesign the organization's offices and received a standard fee for the job. As a promotion tactic, doing such projects at a reduced fee only pays off if you make up for it in publicity and as an item in your promotional materials.

Benefits of Professional Society Work

General information about future project developments that is shared by the network of members.

Specific information from colleagues, for example, on prospective client's organization or cooperativeness and promptness in paying bills.

Referrals within the professioial society of smaller or more specialized jobs from big offices to appropriate colleagues.

Exposure through showhouses, design awards programs, and public service projects such as community design centers, donated ideas for refurbishing Main Street, or a public park.

Professional Societies for Designers National Headquarters

Acoustical Society
of America (ASA)
335 East 45th Street
New York City 10017

American Institute
of Architects (AIA)
1735 New York Avenue, N.W.
Washington, D.C. 20006

American Institute
of Graphic Arts (AIGA)
1059 Third Avenue
New York City 10021

American Planning Association
(APA)
1776 Massachusetts Ave.,
N.W.
Washington, D.C. 20036

American Society of Heating,
Refrigerating
and Air Conditioning Engineers,
Inc. (ASHRAE)
1791 Tullie Circle, N.E.
Atlanta, GA 30329

American Society of
Interior Designers (ASID)
1430 Broadway
New York City 10018

American Society of
Landscape Architects (ASLA)
1733 Connecticut Avenue,
N.W.
Washington, D.C. 20009

Environmental Design
Research Association, Inc. (EDRA)
L'Enfant Plaza Station
P.O. Box 23129
Washington, D.C. 20024

Illuminating Engineering Society
(IES)
345 East 47th Street
New York City 10017

Industrial Design Society
of America (IDSA)
6802 Poplar Place
McLean, VA 22102

Institute of Business Designers
(IBD)
1155 Merchandise Mart
Chicago, IL 60654

International Association of
Lighting Designers (IALD)
40 East 49th Street
New York City 10017

National Council of
Acoustical Consultants (NCAC)
66 Morris Avenue
P.O. Box 359
Springfield, NJ 07081

National Council of
Architectural Registration Boards
(NCARB)
1735 New York Avenue, N.W.
Washington, D.C. 20006

Taking a leadership role in your professional society, however, may be difficult to rationalize in terms of marketing. For large, multipartner design companies, there is enough public relations value in having someone serve as an officer that the lost time is covered. But for small firms, the effort of being president or program chairman for your local group can detract from time better spent on marketing your practice.

DOES IT PAY?

WHEN DOES "public awareness" effort lead to a stronger practice, and when is it just self-indulgence? The only way you can decide whether your public outreach activities are worthwhile to your overall business-creation program is to test each action—whether it is a speech or a year as chairman of the local ASID program committee—against your previously stated plan. If, for instance, an opportunity to speak before a garden club has been tendered, you may have trouble justifying it since your firm is primarily focused on branch banks and stock brokerage offices. With your marketing framework in place, you can not only gracefully deflect irrelevant possibilities, but a marketing plan can help you figure out what kinds of public service work you *should* be doing.

Without a commitment to the professional beliefs and ideals that you have developed over the years, design practice can be a pretty superficial business. Yet you must keep in mind the economic basis for practice. Your marketing program brings the two together. It helps smooth out the ups-and-downs of purely referral practice and offers guidance for day-to-day operation.

Chapter Nine
MARKETING FOR VERY SMALL OFFICES

ALTHOUGH marketing design services on a small budget doesn't necessarily apply only to firms with one or two professionals, there are special problems in marketing if you have to do everything yourself.

Indeed, how do you do the work and market at the same time? In Al De Vido's words, "It seems that most of my time is spent getting the jobs out. I have able assistants, but since I do all the conceptual design, client contact, and most of the administration, it's difficult to block out the time for a planned marketing effort." When he said this, his Manhattan architectural office had a staff of three including a secretary and two drafters.

The definition of a "very small office" varies from one design discipline to another. For the purposes of this chapter, however, a team of one principal and three or four staff at most, or a pair of principals with one or two staff, as in the case of Warren Infield and Frank D'Astolfo, is the upper limit. Thus Judith Chafee, Gail Biddison and Pam Radford, Gordon Perry, Will Ching, Ken Arutunian, and Pamela Waters all represent very small firms whose marketing efforts are necessarily limited.

The picture is hardly grim though. It just means that your time must be carefully planned to allow for regular marketing effort and that you must set realistic marketing goals. Here is where time counts for more than money.

COPING WITH THE CLASSIC DILEMMA

THE MOST IMPORTANT issue for a small firm, in Gail Biddison's words, "is the consistent allocation of time for marketing. It is far too easy for principals of a small firm to shuffle marketing to the back burner. But it is critical to structure time for marketing and then DO IT!"

A test of how serious you are about getting new business is what part of the day or week you put aside for marketing. For most of us, evenings and weekends are the best time for design work because that's when the telephone keeps quiet. Fortunately, marketing is best done during business hours when prospective clients are in their offices. Many of the other operations related to prospecting are most efficiently done during the day: typing and mailing letters and packages of work examples, cold telephone calls, meeting with prospects, trips to show off completed projects or installations.

Yet even with the most meticulous planning, unexpected developments in current projects arise with an urgency that takes precedence over any other work. That's the dilemma. Suddenly it's five o'clock and you didn't get those prospecting calls in. That's why truly realistic quotas for each week must be set. Maybe you don't get around to them until Thursday or Friday, but if it is four or five calls to businesses who recently got a mailing from you, force yourself to cram them into an hour or two—thus getting them over all at once!

If you have always had trouble making this sort of follow-up call, realize most designers have the same problem. Here is Gail Biddison again: "Once contact is made, it takes an enormous amount of time and energy to follow up. Yet this is probably the make-or-break factor in a successful marketing program."

Part of an efficient marketing plan is to be sure that everything the staff (even if it is only part-time student employees) can do is delegated to them. A well-organized system for replying to referrals and inquiries, such as stuffing reprints into a folder and typing a cover letter from an already written example, can be carried out by almost anyone with minimal supervision. Save your own efforts for organizing and personal contact. Thus you will feel, at least, that your own involvement is making some difference.

One way, as an individual practitioner, to help yourself ease into the habit of marketing consistently is to set realistic goals for your program when you begin. Too many designers, when the realization strikes home that they must go looking for work or face serious economic consequences, apply "systems logic" to the problem and soon have a marketing structure so grand that three partners would be needed to carry it out. That quickly leads to no action at all. Thus it is essential for the very small office to pick its targets with care. Go after types of work in which you already have experience. Avoid corporate and government agencies (unless you have extremely solid connections "inside") in favor of other small businesses and organizations where your personal attention to the project will be appreciated. In that way you have some chance of success within six months or a year and you will be encouraged to maintain the marketing habit.

Graphic designers and lighting designers are among those who do many short-term projects. They have to find more jobs per year to keep the business going than do architects or others who get more long-range assignments. Thus Warren Infield and Frank D'Astolfo have to get better results than most of us from the 10 percent of their time they put into marketing. "A typography salesman recently told us," says Infield, "that a 2 percent rate of establishing new accounts is considered very effective in his business. Then only 2 percent of those turn out to be repeat clients. Needless to say our rate is much higher—recommendations from suppliers and referrals from satisfied clients make a lot of difference. We are our best representatives and would never consider hiring someone to make contacts for us."

SELLING THE PERSONAL TOUCH

THE "PERSONAL TOUCH," in fact, is what gives the small office a definite advantage over larger, corporate-style design firms. The challenge is to find those among your potential clients who will appreciate your readiness to provide individualized, comprehensive service. For the same fee that from a large firm might mean standardized and limited response to the project's complexity, they can have your full attention—the principal, instead of a rotating line-up of

Gordon Perry's Greenwich Village loft conveys a spirit of design awareness to his visiting clients. They can see that he is involved in every project his firm carries out.

"associates" and job captains. Jeanne Hartnett finds that it can indeed work to the advantage of a small firm: "We emphasize that 'what they see is what they get.' Clients who have been the 'large firm' route very much appreciate the knowledge that our personnel have been with the firm for a number of years so that continuity is assured."

It is important while detailing the nature of design services to explain to the prospective client that the process is based on one-to-one interaction, that you help the client define the issues, and that you then derive the solution from that study. Many people start out thinking that designers have a sackful of "ideas" that can be altered "while you wait." They must be helped to see the benefits of working along with you for a customized answer to their needs. It can be tricky because Americans are used to quick, ready-made "products" bought off the shelf. Too much "process" talk and they get confused and edgy.

There is another reason to put most of your energy into listening rather than talking when canvassing for prospects. People are flattered that you care about their problems and, as Bill Koster emphasizes, "that begins to build trust, which is what we sell and what clients buy." Gordon Perry puts it this way: "It's a person-to-person relationship and I believe that people make many decisions based on emotional responses. Along those lines, I am very aware that an executive will sometimes ask his secretary for an opinion of a particular visitor. At one time, if a prospect's secretary was a little curt to me, I would give it right back. Not anymore. I try to learn their first name (or their last name if that seems more appropriate) and I use it when I call. They very often have a tremendous influence on their bosses."

OVERCOMING THE "SMALL OFFICE STIGMA"

THE BIGGEST PROBLEM, as we all know, is not doing the work once it is given to us by clients—no matter how big the job may be—but in convincing them that as a small office we can deliver on time and within budget. There are a couple of reasons why large organizations seek out large design firms. First, there is the "corporations-speak-only-to-corporations" phenomenon. Hierarchical business structures operate on the basis of delegated authority. Large design firms, with their selling teams, design teams, and production teams, offer a similar sort of structure and, just as important, a similar style of behavior and appearance on the part of the creative members— no beards, blue jeans, or Stetson hats. A second, more tangible reason is that the corporate project representative needs assurance that no matter what happens to individuals within the design firm, the job will keep moving and there will always be somebody reasonably competent in charge. The one- or two-partner outfit could dissolve and disappear next week for all they know. The common response by designers is the use of free-lance or semi-autonomous specialists who are offered as "John Smith and Associates." That often includes a guided tour through what appears to be a fully-staffed office. No doubt it sometimes works.

The important thing is to emphasize a high level of expertise and a professional approach. "We stress on all jobs our record in budget control," says Ken Arutunian, "and in listing related projects in proposals, we normally list budget and compare it with construction cost." Ed Mills notes, "We present Voorsanger and Mills as a small but growing group whose work is highly creative and professional, promoting the fact that the principals design and manage each project. The potential client understands he will be working with whomever he is interviewing for the entire job." Warren Infield adds, "We have discovered that our compact size and the close attention of both partners to all projects have made us competitive; the direct communication, personal attention, and desire to build client goodwill enable us to win accounts that value these qualities over size, reputation, and back-up staff."

The small design practice offers a vitality that can benefit clients of all magnitudes, but especially those businesses small enough to be run by the individuals that founded them or by a small group of partners. They are the sort of business people who appreciate the service and personal commitment that someone like you brings to a job.

Things to Do

Make marketing your highest priority and sell it to everyone on your staff.

Appoint one principal to be in charge of marketing, the "head cheerleader."

Choose an appropriate level of promotion and sales activity and aim for it every week.

Hold frequent, at least weekly, supportive reporting sessions to monitor progress of the program.

Decide to "do a few things well"—whether that means specialization or just clear limits on the types of projects your firm accepts.

Transfer as much marketing support work to your staff as possible.

Have a staff member search relevant newspapers and business magazines for work opportunities.

Keep in touch with former clients and other business acquaintances—don't be timid about asking them for help in marketing.

Things to Avoid

Relying on referrals for future work—sitting back and waiting for the telephone to ring.

Promoting and selling only when the office needs another job or when you can't think of anything else to do.

Sharing profits with members of the firm who won't participate in marketing.

Becoming impatient when your marketing program fails to pay off after six months or a year of effort.

Preparing government RFPs (including 254/255 forms) for jobs you have little chance of winning.

Giving free lectures to audiences whose members are unlikely to make use of your professional services in the future.

Borrowing money for promotion against future income you assume it will generate.

Jordan/Mitchell

1920 Chestnut Street,
Philadelphia, Pennsylvania 19103

Architecture, planning, interior design

Established: 1981

Staff (1983): Two principals,
eight project architects, two
administrators

Educational Background:
Joe J. Jordan, FAIA:
B. Arch., University of Illinois;
James E. Mitchell, AIA:
A.B., M.S. (Physics), Harvard;
M.Arch., University of Pennsylvania

Professional Society:
Mitchell: Affiliate member, American
Society of Heating,
Refrigeration and Air-Conditioning
Engineers, Inc. (ASHRAE)
Chairman, AIA National Committee
on Computers & Architecture

Joe J. Jordan   James E. Mitchell

PROFESSIONAL FRAMEWORK.
Both Joe Jordan and Jim Mitchell
were in practice by themselves when
they decided to join forces. Jordan
contributed more than twenty years
of experience in gerontological projects (facilities for the elderly) and a
strong design reputation. Mitchell
brought an extensive knowledge of
medical facility design, technical
skills in energy management and
computers, as well as business management abilities. As a prelude to the
union, they had a number of meetings to evaluate each other's
strengths and weaknesses and negotiate the new deal. "We discussed
each of the nine factors [discussed on
pages 15 through 19] individually
and found, to no great surprise, that
we felt similarly on virtually all of
them. One or the other of us felt
competent in each of the requisite
areas," says Jim Mitchell. They decided to aim for a staff of twenty within
five years; two years after starting up,
they had grown from four to ten people. Medical and gerontological
facilities remain their specialties,
with emphasis on project management capabilities. That is a natural
combination for the Philadelphia
region, as elsewhere in the northeast, where an aging population
must be housed and cared for by government and private agencies with
limited budgets.

GOALS AND OBJECTIVES. Goals for
the joint firm grew out of independent statements, prepared by the

future partners, that were compared
and amalgamated. Instead of ranking
them, however, Jordan and Mitchell
agreed to put enrichment of design
quality, client service, and cost control forward as their primary goals—
in short, to increase their professional credibility. Growth and
profitability will benefit, they believe,
as the new firm's strengths are recognized. For a firm that specializes
as tightly as Jordan/Mitchell (J/M),
credibility is the vehicle that will
increase their share of the two markets over the next few years.

MARKETING STRATEGY. Jordan
and Mitchell decided from the beginning to specialize and to aim at
becoming what some would call a
"fairly large" design office. "What
distinguishes our firm from many
other smaller offices," they say, "is
our organized approach and our persistence." Jordan/Mitchell makes
regular use of the telephone to gain
personal access to prospects they
identify by research and by reading
trade journals. "We have also bene-
fited from extensive use of the
microcomputer to assist in our marketing effort. It has enabled us to
reach out to many more prospects
than would otherwise be possible."

PROMOTION TACTICS. It is the
microcomputer, indeed, that distinguishes Jordan/Mitchell from
most of the other designers included
here who are serious about promoting and selling their design services.
No doubt because it was a prior
interest of Jim Mitchell's (as one-
time Chairman of the AIA's National

RDAN/MITCHELL, INC.
hitecture, Planning, Interior Design
0 Chestnut Street
iadelphia, Pennsylvania 19103

Mercer Regional Medical Group Office:

Location: Trenton, New Jersey
Client: Mercer Regional Medical Gro

Committee on Computers), the new firm has shaped its marketing efforts around the microcomputer. In the Appendix devoted to them Jordan/Mitchell's experiences are described in detail. Although microcomputers and wordprocessors do not yet fall into the "marketing-on-a-small-budget" category, Mitchell is very enthusiastic about them. "Any designer with more than a couple of people on staff can benefit from using a computer," he says. "In marketing, especially, you are missing an opportunity to increase what you can do."

PROMOTION MATERIALS. Partly because of the typesetting capability of their computer, Jordan and Mitchell have concentrated on printed promotion materials for interviews and presentations with only occasional use of slides. They have compiled printed (not just typed) lists of current work and clients in general and in their specialties, of past work in the specialties of conferences and publications, and of honors or awards they've won. Along with these and especially attractive biography sheets for the principals, Jordan/Mitchell has developed a cost-effective photocard. On glossy card stock

---

Gerontological Planning

JORDAN/MITCHELL, INC.

Architecture, Planning, Interior Design
1600 Chestnut Street
Philadelphia, Pennsylvania 19103
Telephone: (215) 567-4894

Research and Publications

THE AGE OF THE AGING — ELDERLY HOUSING. Contributing consultant to an article in Progressive Architecture Magazine, August 1981.

2.5 MILLION DOLLAR SENIOR CENTER OPENS ITS DOORS IN JACKSONVILLE, FLORIDA. Article in Older American News, published by the U. S. Department of Health and Human Services, September 1980.

DESIGNING INTERIORS FOR THE ELDERLY. Article in Executive Housekeeper Magazine, August 1979.

SENIOR CENTER DESIGN — AN ARCHITECT'S DISCUSSION OF FACILITY PLANNING. Publication for the National Council on the Aging, Inc., 1978.

SENIOR CENTER DESIGN — A BOOK REVIEW. Article in the AIA Journal, November 1978.

RECOGNIZING AND DESIGNING FOR THE SPECIAL NEEDS OF THE ELDERLY. Article in the AIA Journal, September 1977.

SENIOR CENTER FACILITIES — AN ARCHITECT'S EVALUATION OF BUILDINGS, FURNISHINGS AND EQUIPMENT. Publication of the National Council on the Aging, Inc. 1975.

WHAT KIND OF FACILITIES SHALL WE PLAN FOR THE AGING? Article in THE MODERN HOSPITAL, 1957.

Planning Consultation

DOWNTOWN JACKSONVILLE SENIOR CENTER — JACKSONVILLE, FL. Services included establishing community participation, service/space programs, information resource to the design architects plus design and document review. Client: City of Jacksonville.

BALTIMORE COUNTY SENIOR CENTER — BALTIMORE, MD. Consultation in service and space projects as part of feasibility study. Project was completed in 1978 for Nelson-Salabes Architects.

PASSAIC SENIOR CENTER — PASSAIC, NJ. Services involved estimating project size, attendance projections, service and space programming, and design review of preliminary plans. Client: City of Passaic. Completed in 1977.

ELDERADO SENIOR CENTER — PITTSBURGH, PA. Consultation consisted of facility assessment, space programming, serving as a resource to the design architect and design review. Client: Elderado Senior Center. Work completed in 1976.

WILMINGTON SENIOR CENTER — WILMINGTON, DE. A detailed program of space requirements for the renovation and expansion of the center involving preservation of 18th Century historic buildings. Client: The Wilmington Senior Center.

UPPER SHORE AGING, INC. — CENTREVILLE, MD. Development of a feasibility study in a five county area of the rural Upper Eastern Shore for the conversion of public buildings to senior centers.

OHIO PRESBYTERIAN HOMES — WORTHINGTON, OH. Continuing consultation services on the programming and design of commons facilities as part of seven retirement communities throughout the state.

DEPARTMENT OF PARKS, RECREATION AND CULTURAL AFFAIRS — ESSEX COUNTY, NJ. A Work Program to guide the development of a Long Range Plan governing services and facilities for the elderly.

Jordan/Mitchell mount photographs on printed cards (opposite page below) with type set by their own microcomputer. These are used individually or bound into proposals and reports. Typical package of promotion materials includes staff biographies, lists of current projects (opposite page above), lectures and publications (above), awards, and project illustrations (below).

(8½ × 11), descriptive titles are printed in predetermined typefaces and sizes. Then an inexpensive 8 × 10 color enlargement from a slide photograph is cropped and mounted in the space above. The resulting exhibit can be used by itself or bound into a proposal. All this constitutes a system that allows J/M to assemble a professional looking portfolio of promotional materials quickly for a reasonable cost.

EVALUATION. Even though Jordan and Mitchell have gone through the steps in planning their marketing program, they have found it difficult to meet the quotas for prospect contact that they have set for themselves. Twelve hours a week to be spent on marketing by each principal is their goal, and yet because of the need to oversee and develop projects already commissioned that is difficult to meet. The irony is that even a modest promotional effort only pays off when you actually make that personal contact with a prospect.

Gere Kavanaugh Designs

420 Boyd Street,
Los Angeles, California 90013
Architectural interiors and color,
graphics, product development,
exhibitions

Established: 1966

Staff (1983): Principal, two architects,
two graphic designers,
artist/graphic designer, secretary

Educational Background:
B.A., Memphis Academy of Arts;
M.F.A., Cranbrook Academy of Art

Teaching Position:
Visiting Professor,
University of Southern California
(Introductory course in Architectural
Interiors)

Professional Societies:
Affiliate member, American
Institute of Architects;
Board member, California Design;
Board member, Craft and Folk Art
Museum (Los Angeles)

PROFESSIONAL FRAMEWORK.
Here is a design practice that can
properly be called a studio: small,
informal, and focused on the "art" of
design. The original and the innovative are Gere Kavanaugh's
specialties in design. She likes the
kinds of jobs that other interior firms
do not seek: household accessories
such as dishes and tableware (not to
forget the table itself), fabrics, and
decorative graphics. Yet Kavanaugh
also does urban-scale projects such
as subway station interiors and architectural graphics. For a huge multi-
use project in Beverly Hills, she has
done the color program and added
the humanizing details that architects sometimes forget. Her office is
in an old building on the edge of
downtown Los Angeles ("Little
Tokyo"), well placed to keep in touch
with designer friends throughout the
metropolitan region.

GOALS AND OBJECTIVES. She
insists that her primary business goal
is "to do what I like best." That is an
impulse with which any designer can
identify. Yet from a marketing standpoint, it is probably the hardest road
to follow. Projections of workloads,
staff, and space needs are impossible,
let alone forecasting future profits. A
studio operation, like Kavanaugh's,
however, seems better suited to this
business approach than a bigger
practice would be.

MARKETING STRATEGY. In the
past, publication has been an important element in Kavanaugh's efforts
to tell people about her work. Like so
many designers outside New York,
but especially those in the west, she

Gere Kavanaugh

Kavanaugh's work ranges from
furniture design (table for Images of
America shown above) to interiors, such
as The Orange Tree Restaurant in a Los
Angeles department store shown at the
right. Multicolored, random-pattern
ceramic tile floors are one of her
trademarks.

has experienced the sluggishness of the design press in responding to influences and ideas other than the ones in fashion at the moment. Gradually, however, she has realized that those precious design magazine pieces accomplish very little by themselves. Only when they are used to contact people do they become valuable to the designer. Kavanaugh's marketing strategy has evolved into maintaining telephone contact with designer colleagues and former clients—networking. She takes an active role in the Pacific Design Center's annual "West Week" meetings, for instance, because it gives her a chance to renew connections with people who have sent prospects to her in the past.

PROMOTION TACTICS. Personal contact is the heart of Gere Kavanaugh's approach to practice. It is carefully focused on business development, however. "You've got to get the word out to the clients, making it very clear what you can do for *them*," she says, emphasizing the last word. "Don't be vague or offer too many alternatives. It boils down to how you can specifically help the client make money." Kavanaugh recalls phoning a former client, now a major developer, for whom she once did some residential design. "He was still thinking of me on that scale. Yet when I told him about my current work, things as complex as what he is doing, he was happy to make the connection."

EVALUATION. Gere Kavanaugh is a "designer's designer." Many of her jobs come through the wide circle of acquaintances she keeps up. Design has been less a business to her than a way of life. Her strength has been in creative problem solving. Success in that has brought a reasonably steady succession of projects over the years. A small, informal office has allowed her to focus on each job as it came along.

In mid-1983 she began reviewing her client files to work out a more systematic approach to future commissions. To begin with, she is putting completed projects into categories. Then she can decide which ones have been the most successful and deserve further market development. Whatever marketing decisions she makes will probably involve direct telephone contact. Kavanaugh believes the key to success in promoting and selling design services is to let people know you want to work for them. "The bottom line is guts, persistence, just following through all the time. And being out there selling. The big guys are out there every day. They make the contacts years before the prospect realizes he will need design services. Naturally, when the client is ready he turns to the firm he knows about. There's plenty to learn from the big offices about marketing. Talk to your friends who work there; find out how they do it. A lot of their techniques will work for you."

Koster and Holzheimer, Architects Inc.

1220 West Sixth Street,
Cleveland, Ohio 44113

Municipal facilities, recreation centers, libraries

Established: Koster and Associates, 1963;
Koster and Holzheimer, 1976

Staff (1983): Two principals,
two project architects,
marketing coordinator, secretary

Educational Background:
William D. Koster: B.S. (architecture),
University of Cincinnati;
David L. Holzheimer: B.Arch.,
Case Western Reserve University;
Sandra J. Bolek: B.A.,
Cleveland State University

Professional Society:
Holzheimer: President (1984),
Cleveland Chapter,
American Institute of Architects

Photo: Peter Renerts Photographer

William D. Koster   David L. Holzheimer

Handsome, functional public buildings such as this fire station in Bay Village, Ohio, have helped Koster and Holzheimer develop a strong reputation among elected officials over a large marketing area.

PROFESSIONAL FRAMEWORK. Bill Koster and David Holzheimer have a marketing plan, a full-time marketing coordinator, Sandy Bolek, and Koster estimates that he spends 56 percent of his time on it. But the key to new business development for this small design office is their Board of Directors. Along with the two partners, two Cleveland businessmen (one with no design background at all) meet at least quarterly to review and critique marketing and project management progress (see page 20). From the landmark Old Arcade built in 1896, full of architects' offices, Koster and Holzheimer moved in 1981 to a loft building in what is left of Cleveland's warehouse district. What made the move attractive was four times the floor area for the same rent they had been paying. It offers them the opportunity to grow slowly, as their marketing efforts pay off, without worrying about where to put new staff.

GOALS AND OBJECTIVES. "Without a successful marketing plan economic stability cannot be achieved and professional excellence is denied to a firm," says Koster. His primary goal therefore has been to build and maintain an experienced staff. These individuals, sharing his standards for design and client service, could grow professionally and personally within the framework of an established practice as is the custom among lawyers, for instance. These personnel-oriented goals support Koster and Holzheimer's objective of maintaining their expertise in at least three work categories or building types—municipal facilities, recreation centers, and

libraries—over a long period of time. Consistent profitability will result, in their opinion, from the businesslike pursuit of these goals through marketing.

MARKETING STRATEGY. Sandy Bolek had been Koster's secretary and bookkeeper for a long time, holding the practice togther through thick and thin. Thus it was a logical step in 1978 to give her the full-time job of coordinating the marketing work. She already knew more about the business than anyone else. Making use of a market research program that monitors job potential in fifty-six of Ohio's counties, she has established herself with hundreds of contacts. A promising telephone conversation generates a letter that is then followed by another call. Bolek sets up meetings for Koster with the municipal and library board officials who are contemplating projects for future bond issues. When he meets with these people, Koster helps them work out the financial feasibility of their proposals. Then the municipality or library board can decide whether the bond issue will win at the polls a year or two later. Here Koster sees the beginning of the design process. Furthermore, when the money does become available, his firm, he feels, has long before earned the trust of the new project's stewards.

PROMOTION TACTICS. Koster and Holzheimer sometimes track a possible job for several years. When it is a prospect that they particularly want, they develop a marketing plan just for that commission. The key to their success is follow-up. "At one point,"

Photo: Peter Renerts Photographer

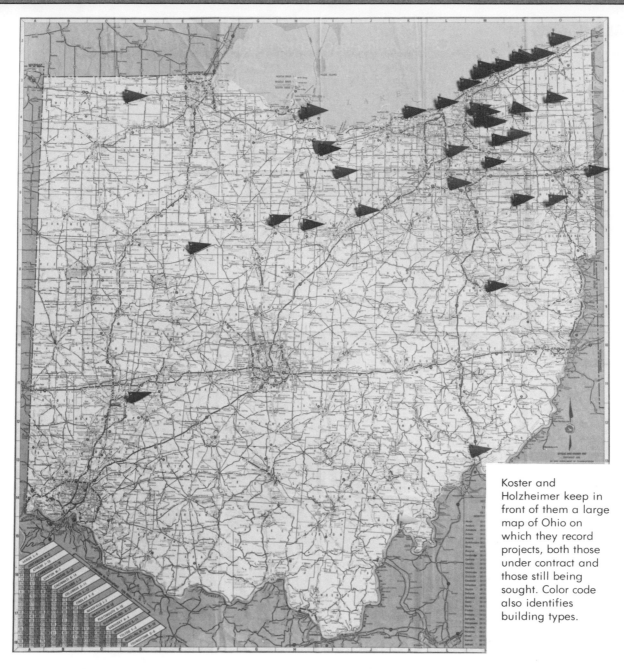

Koster and Holzheimer keep in front of them a large map of Ohio on which they record projects, both those under contract and those still being sought. Color code also identifies building types.

says Koster, "we had six jobs on the boards that wouldn't be there if we had given up after the first contact." By recognizing, in the specialties they've chosen—municipal buildings, for example—that potential clients need help in working through the financial implications of their plans, Koster and Holzheimer learned how to capture prospects' attention. That's what marketing is for.

PROMOTION MATERIALS. Ten or fifteen years ago, when Koster was practicing by himself, he developed elaborate printed brochures and

folders to describe his completed projects. These days the firm uses in-house graphic techniques exclusively (so that materials can be quickly developed which focus on the specific prospect's project). A Kroy lettering machine, a photocopier, and markers on tracing paper (used in an overhead projector) are their presentation media today. The main effort goes into "lots of phone research, a meeting with the prospect, and a visit to the site," says Koster and Holzheimer. "Then with our simple tools, we produce a carefully thought-out presentation of how we will solve *their* problem."

EVALUATION. "Above all," they say, "TRUST is what we sell and trust is what the clients buy." So many librarians were calling the Ohio Library Association (OLA) to check out Koster and Holzheimer that the organization itself decided to find out who these architects were. From that interview came a request for the firm to lead two all-day workshops on library restoration at OLA conferences. Koster and Holzheimer came home from the first workshop with four more library jobs to add to the ten or twelve they already were doing.

Gordon Randall Perry Design

121 West Third Street,
New York City 10012

Product and packaging design

Established: 1976

Staff (1983): Principal, two designers,
three free-lance designers,
one clerical (part-time)

Educational Background:
B.I.D., M.I.D., Pratt Institute

Teaching Position:
Visiting Assistant Professor, Pratt

Professional Society:
Treasurer, New York Chapter,
Industrial Design Society of America
(IDSA)

Gordon Randall Perry

PROFESSIONAL FRAMEWORK.
Gordon Perry characterizes his practice as a business that has evolved through trial and error. Yet Perry has had a sense of where he was going all along. He has understood that if his firm was to remain small, then he had to develop credentials that would attract significant commissions in spite of his size. He points out that as a design office grows, the importance of personnel as a factor in its success "becomes extremely critical. Good staff is hard to put together. The design profession seems to attract a great many strange people. While they may be very talented and gifted, I never cease to be amazed at their ability to create havoc in an organization." Yet every designer will empathize with Perry when he says, "Eventually, I

would like to grow bigger and have two or three senior people under me so I can afford to get away from the business for short vacations."
At present, Gordon's office is in his Greenwich Village loft, a soaring duplex that looks like the set for a movie about a designer. His living quarters overlook the main floor where drafting tables are fitted around the twenty-foot high ficus tree and other plants. When a big push is on, those tables are occupied by industrial design students from Pratt Institute.

GOALS AND OBJECTIVES. Perry has a fifteen-year plan with three major goals: First to gain the recognition that will enable him to tap sources of work for which an unknown designer would not be con-

The pasta machine designed for Osrow Products (right) is able to produce a wide range of dough-based foods from spaghetti to tortillas. Perry has used pictures of it on mailing fliers and as reprints taken from articles featuring the machine. Perry-designed electronic equipment workstations (opposite page above) include this IMS furniture system for Home Furniture. Such photos are useful for publicity. Perry's redesign of the familiar Higgins drawing ink bottle (opposite page below) returns to the wide-shouldered shape of the original.

sidered. Second "to be able to make money easier, that is, to spend much less time looking for work so I can focus on jobs that will make me money." Third to have "the financial security to go after jobs that interest and excite me." Now working on goal number two, he see his immediate objectives to be "increased credibility to the business community" and higher fees.

MARKETING STRATEGY. Product designers, unlike designers in most of the other disciplines, focus on an easily identified market. Manufacturers of specific items are not only listed in trade directories but gather once or twice a year at shows, often in Chicago but occasionally in some other city. That gives the designer who is marketing to them an opportunity to meet and become acquainted with these producers under conditions that are informal yet dedicated to developing new business. Perry presents himself

personally and through modest advertisements in the directories published for the trade show. Even such a tight market requires analysis, however. "Many of these manufacturers are so small that they can't afford to pay a designer. That means I have to cross-reference them through a financial directory. Then I code them according to location, type of product, etc., so I can prepare a marketing letter that is specifically for them."

PROMOTION TACTICS. Perry's telephone sales technique is described in detail on page 100. He recognizes that a cold call is the beginning of a serious selling effort. Even if nine calls seem unproductive, the tenth may be timed just right. If for the tenth time you can express in your conversation a sincere interest in helping the company you've called, an interview might be granted. Gordon Perry has learned how to send energy and enthusiasm through the telephone wires so that face-to-face contact results. His advice is, "Learn to love the telephone."

PROMOTION MATERIALS. When Perry prepares for an interview, he has learned to stock his portfolio or slideshow with not just work that he knows his prospect will want to see but a few pictures that illustrate the entire range of his work. "When you are selling and showing your work, address the person's problems as closely as you can. Don't present your work as an abstraction. It's got to be applied work, even though it may not be a direct solution to his or her problem. If you can relate to them by the way you talk, then the prospect will relate to you."

EVALUATION. Gordon Perry reaches out to find work in an effective way partly because he has developed a system for keeping track of his contacts. "When I started out, I didn't think much of schedules and checklists. As the complexity of my work and the size of my staff has grown, I have learned that such tools are valuable indeed. Until I accepted the necessity for this kind of organization, I wasted a good deal of time running my projects that I can now spend looking for new business."

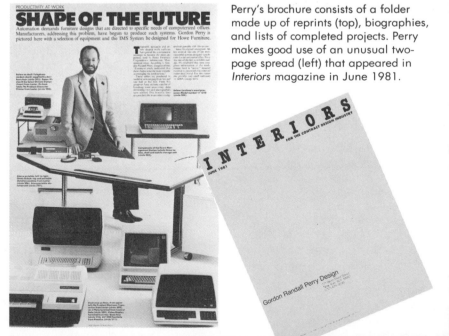

Perry's brochure consists of a folder made up of reprints (top), biographies, and lists of completed projects. Perry makes good use of an unusual two-page spread (left) that appeared in *Interiors* magazine in June 1981.

Part Four

FOCUSING YOUR EFFORTS

IF THE FIRST PARTS of this book are akin to conceptualizing and developing a design solution, this one, "Focusing Your Efforts," is like doing working drawings and writing specs or pasting up the mechanical. It isn't easy to make it sound like fun. Yet every serious architect or designer knows that without responsible and dedicated attention to the endless details of documenting a job, quality results are impossible.

Marketing works exactly the same way. Your previous efforts at isolating goals, designing a marketing plan, and researching your business development possibilities have an excitement about them that is, in a way, satisfying without any further action—just as a set of attractive renderings has its own life. But like your best design efforts, all this marketing preparation is only too likely to get stalled if you do not *will* it into reality. Yes, designers push their projects toward existence; not infrequently it is the designer's enthusiasm that overcomes inertia caused by client uncertainty, financing problems, or technical difficulties. That's why the steps spelled out on the next pages deserve your study and then your commitment to carrying out the ones that seem appropriate to your marketing plan. Not just for six months to "try it out," but for the next two or three years.

Chapter Ten
MAKING CONTACT

TO DESIGNERS AND other professionals, the hardest part of marketing seems to be the act of reaching out to others. Is it pride? Is it shyness? Is it fear that makes us so reluctant to "go out after a sale"? In fact, it is a human inhibition to resist asking for help, to fear rejection. Therefore we are not so much different than everyone else.

Keep in mind that most people look at designers and architects with considerable respect. If the person you call isn't interested in design services at the time, it doesn't mean that they won't receive the call graciously. Business people who have had experience seeking prospects by telephone are often quite sympathetic to the caller. Often they will, given the opportunity, chat a bit rather than answer curtly and hang up. A systematic approach to making contacts is important because it reinforces the necessity of persistence in marketing. If you know you must make five calls today no matter what, it is a lot easier to dial the second call after getting nowhere on the first one.

MASTERING
COLD CALLS

THERE IS NO MORE effective way to explore markets that are essentially unknown to you than the telephone. Whether the call is truly "cold"—meaning no prior acquaintance with your firm—or has been warmed up a bit with a mailing, it is the best means of determining interest from a prospective client.

Naturally your chance of getting through on the first try to the person who can respond authoritatively to your questions is small. But that merely makes clear that your telephoning campaign must be designed to elicit responses at each stage that lead you closer to the right person. Be prepared to make a number of calls to each source you've identified with the intention of building the interest a little bit each time. The goal, then, is to find out what the needs are at the other end of the phone so that the next call can be shaped constructively to meet them.

It is a challenge to the person making cold calls to sense when even the smallest positive response has been offered. The trick is to draw the other person into a conversation by asking for information about the business. By asking questions about the company you have reached rather than giving a speech about your firm's virtues, you are actually beginning to sell, to convince them of your interest in solving their problem.

Checklist of Telephone Style Tips

Be polite even though the response may be curt or rude.

Speak clearly so that the other person does not have to ask you to repeat what you said.

Plan your statement so it is concise and logical in order.

Use a light-hearted tone of voice so that the person called feels some pleasure from your call; smile while you are talking.

Offer enthusiastic and positive response to whatever expression of interest comes from the other end of the line.

Have well-informed, thoughtful answers to questions that might be raised.

Remember, you believe in what you are selling—not every salesperson has that luxury.

Sample Telemarketing Script

Note: The following six negative "first answers" to your opening statement include an appropriate response requesting an appointment. The three negative "second answers" might follow any of your responses to the "first answer."

Opening: "Hello, I'm Michael Mickey of Mickey, Hickey and Dickey, Industrial Designers. I'm asking for an appointment to show you how we can help you increase profits."

Possible First Answer: "We're not interested."
Response: "Are you aware of the financial benefits that can come from redesigning an established line of merchandise like your desk accessories (based on prior research)? May I come over next week to show you some of our case studies? Is Wednesday morning free for you?"

Possible First Answer: "We're not in the market right now. Maybe in six months. . . ."
Response: "There's nothing like planning ahead. Let me come over next week and discuss how we can help you with inexpensive marketing and feasibility studies. They'll make it easy to begin producing a new line when the economy picks up. When are you available?

Possible First Answer: "I'm too busy right now to see you."
Response: "Glad things are going along so well for you. Maybe we can ease the load a bit by helping you restructure your product line. Can I have ten minutes next week to show you how we worked with Widget, Inc. (in the same field) to increase their profits?"

Possible First Answer: "We've already got a designer."
Response: "Have you thought about the advantages of fresh input on your product design? I think you'll like our approach. Can you spare a few minutes next week to talk it over?"

Possible First Answer: "We haven't had very good luck with designers in the past."
Response: "We specialize in first-class client service, as you'll see when I show you the endorsements from other companies we've worked for. Can I come over next week and share them with you? What's a good day for you?"

Possible Second Answer: "Look, I just don't have time next week."
Response: "OK, I'll send you our portfolio instead. Then I'll get back to you in a couple of weeks after you've had a chance to browse through it. Let me make sure I've got your correct title and address. . . ."

Possible Second Answer: "I can't offer you any work—it's not worth your time."
Response: "Don't worry about that; I'm going to be coming over there sometime next week anyway. Tell me when it's convenient for you and I'll fit this other errand in then."

Possible Second Answer: "I really hate it when somebody is as pushy as you are over the telephone!"
Response: "I'm sorry I upset you so! It's just that I *really* believe we can do a good job for you. Let me send you some material on the firm and you decide for yourself, OK?"

The telemarketing script (left) includes responses you can use to six possible negative first answers by the prospect, as well as answers to three negative second responses.

Ultimately, as Will Ching puts it, you are after a "face-to-face meeting." Jordan/Mitchell, which generally uses the telephone as its initial contact tool (although they have tried prior mailings as well), strives for a personal interview as soon as possible when calling organizations in their specialties. Gordon Perry says: "It sometimes takes five or six calls to get through. But now I'm on the phone with the executive. His time is short and I have to make my impact quickly. I'm friendly but perhaps a bit chameleonlike since I'm being very sensitive to that person and responding in a way that I hope he or she will be interested in hearing. Typically I get, 'Well, we're interested but not now.' Or, 'Well, we're not interested right now but give us six months or a year.' In a small percentage of calls, I will hear, 'Yes, things are cooking, why don't we arrange to get together and let me see your work.' That's all I need."

Follow-up on cold calls can be either more calls, as just noted, or a letter. Bill Koster says: "We have learned that each phone call must precipitate a letter and each letter a meeting and so on until we are commissioned for a study or the entire project." In any case, it is follow-up that makes the difference between successful marketing and a token effort.

Let's face it, many designers have an aversion to asking for work over the telephone. First there is a fear of bothering people. Maybe you are someone who feels annoyed when the telephone rings and the caller is looking for a job or trying to sell you something. But most of us, assuming the caller is polite, don't mind terribly getting such calls. Put yourself in the other person's place. That's the way to overcome the sense that whomever you call seeking new business will be unhappy: chances are, they will behave the way you do.

Second there is the fear of being rejected. Some people have a genuine, psychological problem there, but again for most of us, it is a momentary concern and doesn't send us into an emotional tailspin. Just remember that when you have to say "no" to the individual who calls with a request you can't fulfill, you probably feel a bit sad. Let the person whom you called carry whatever burden he or she will. Your reason for calling is honorable and even essential to the health of your business, thus no cause for any more emotional input than absolutely necessary.

Telephone style can be analyzed and developed just like any other skill. Practice it with your marketing-support person or with a friend who knows something about telephone sales. Joe Jordan learned about cold calls from his insurance salesman. Learn to be direct and positive with an emphasis on enthusiastic interest in the circumstance of the company or person you have called. A telephone script (see sample in box on page 99) may be useful for getting past the first difficult moments, but it is not meant as a framework for every call you make. If you can learn to draw people out during the call, even make them laugh, you may learn to enjoy making cold calls, and your chances of success will increase.

MAKING CANVASSING VISITS COUNT

THERE IS A difference between an interview and a canvassing visit. An interview occurs with the full assent and commitment of the person or group you are going to see. A canvassing visit, on the other hand, is a bit like a cold call in that it may be somewhat unexpected. Yet there are times when it is a worthwhile way to use your marketing energies. If you have gotten a small expression of interest on a cold call, if you have a solid lead based on research or a

---

Let Your Prospects Teach You

The important thing is not what you do with marketing; it is what marketing does with you. If you sit in your office dreaming your dreams and waiting for the phone to ring, you stop growing. If you get out and ask people what they want, what they need, you gradually come to perceive better what your job ought to be. And being a designer, a problem-solver, you'll figure out how to fulfill their needs in a way that is comfortable, even exciting for you. It may take a couple of years, but you will have evolved, through marketing, into a better—and certainly busier—professional.

phone call from someone in your "network," or if you have had a referral from a source that indicates it is all right to "just drop in" on the interested party, pick up your portfolio and go! There are many times when you are going past the prospect's office anyway and have, as an excuse, the obligation that brought you into the neighborhood.

How much can you accomplish on such a visit? Sometimes you won't get past the executive's secretary or even the receptionist. But by planting a favorable impression there (and maybe even learning a bit about the prospect's plans) you can probably wangle an interview later with the boss, already somewhat informed about company needs. Most salespeople, in fact, assume they will make five calls on a prospect before getting an order.

When you do get in to see the appropriate person, you have a splendid opportunity to begin shaping the project. Instead of trotting out a full-dress exhibit of your wares, spend the time getting the prospect to muse about how, when the job actually does firm up, he or she will go about carrying it out. Ask questions that help the executive understand more clearly the complications of such a project, offer thoughts about relevant techniques and relative costs, suggest sources of information, financing, possible design directions, and so on. To use Pamela Waters' phrase, this is an opportunity for "professional generosity." She, in fact, goes so far as to suggest other designers whom she feels might be more appropriate in the specific case. But, as her experience has proven, it is a time for planting the seeds of trust in you that can later sprout into valuable work. Here, in a sense, is the difference between "promoting" and "selling." Visits such as these are developing future business that could not be obtained by an immediate sales presentation.

Another possibility, on such a visit, is to ask the person you have met about other prospects in his or her business field. Obviously, that is not the first item to bring up, but if the conversation has proceeded well and the interviewee seems comfortable with you, the potential for hooking into a new network is there for the asking. As noted earlier, business people are usually less shy than designers about discussing deals and prospects in their field of interest. You can benefit from it.

Needless to say, follow-up on productive canvassing visits is crucial. Keep in touch with the prospect every three to six months as appropriate. Let him or her know the results of any lead that may have been offered. If there is a genuine possibility of a project within the next year, ask for an opportunity when the time comes to present your credentials to the designer review committee. One or two such visits each week offer the possibility of marketing pay-off within the first year.

DEVELOPING
MAILING PROGRAMS

DESIGNERS, compared with most businesses using direct mail marketing, have a relatively small audience. Instead of millions of pieces—or even 100,000—you are probably going to send out a thousand mailings maximum each year. Therefore the techniques used and the material prepared will be a good deal more selective than most of what appears in our mailboxes these days. Nonetheless, "mass mailing" is not popular with most designers who fear that such an approach might compromise their "professional image." There are more personalized methods, however, that easily overcome this objection (see chart on page 102). The important thing to remember, says Ann Boyar, whatever the level of mailing activity you choose, is that it has to be maintained over two or three years before you decide it is not working.

Mailing Program Elements

Category	Description	Annual Quantity	Frequency	Source and Annual Requirements of New Names
General Mailing	Tearsheets, articles about firm, project updates, Christmas cards, and so on	1,000+	Twice a year	Mailing list based on former clients, friends of the firm, recent acquaintances: 50 new names per year
Newsletter	Two or more printed pages with photos, project description material, articles on subjects related to practice, news of awards, new colleagues, and so forth	1,000+	Quarterly or every four months	Same mailing list as above but also selected names from cold calling program, selected names from professional directories, and so on: 200 new names per year
Descriptive Folder	Sized for a #10 envelope, one printed page (both sides) focusing on one of the firm's specialties: nursing home ideas or "new concepts in fast food outlets"	1,000+	50 per week	Unselected names from mailing lists or business directories: 2,500 names per year and also advertising leads
General Letters	Standard form letter with specific information about firm that is individually typed or done on a word processor	1,000+ to 1,500	20 to 30 per week	Selected names from mailing lists or directories: If one out of every five names is used, 5,000 to 6,000 names
Specific Letters	Personalized letter that can be based on a standard form but responding to a specific situation with firm's credentials in that field	500	10 per week	Leads gotten from newspaper, other printed sources, or vague leads: 500 new names per year
Cover letters with Portfolio or Brochure	Personalized letter that refers to the source from which the lead came and specific job and asks for interview	150	3 per week	Solid leads from cold calls, referrals, general and specific letters, canvassing visits, and so forth
Follow-up Letters	Personalized letter referring to a specific marketing action such as: cold call of 6 months earlier, recent visit, and so on	500	10 per week	Based on specific marketing actions such as cold calls, referrals, specific letters, canvassing visits, and so on

A wide variety of mailing options is available to every design firm. While the large-volume techniques seldom produce jobs on their own, they can be valuable in preparing prospects for more personalized follow-up.

Remember the 80/20 rule: Eighty percent of the effort usually generates only 20 percent of the rewards. But if you don't do all of it, you probably won't get the 80 percent of rewards that come from the 20 percent of the work either!

A mailing program can be an in-house labor-intensive endeavor that keeps your name in front of a rather large audience without spending a great deal of money: It may be the special effort that brings relatively small results but which reinforces personal contacts and helps them to pay off.

The accompanying chart lists seven specific elements of a mailing program. No firm will use all of them, but combinations of two or three are very effective. The frequencies are given to indicate a maximum practical effort in each category for a small design firm and to give an idea of relative proportion between them.

Jeanne Hartnett's firm follows the program in the accompanying box.

ENTERTAINING AS MARKETING

DESIGNERS GENERALLY look down upon "marketing by entertainment." If that's how you feel, think it over. People do respond warmly to that kind of attention and remember it. Money spent on meals and theater can pay marketing dividends years later. Yet even this need not be expensive. Judith Chafee has developed lunches in the drafting room into her primary business-building technique: "It is difficult for a single woman to entertain for marketing purposes. The ability to entertain in the office, which we do a great deal, provides a natural, generous atmosphere that cannot yet be achieved in our society by a woman asking a man to lunch, even at an appropriate and expensive club. Our lunches also contribute to staff involvement in marketing and strengthen our relationships with contractors, engineers, and others." Chafee also has a Christmas party for clients and colleagues.

Parties thrown by your firm at times of the year when social life is a bit slow—to celebrate Frank Lloyd Wright's birthday (June 8) or the anniversary of hanging up your shingle—will no doubt be well attended. Consider asking clients, upon completion of a major project, to gather their friends and business acquaintances to "christen" it. That can work as well for graphic design commissions as for interior design or architectural jobs.

Jeanne Hartnett's Marketing Program

1. Send brochure with letter introducing the firm to a specific lead gotten from a referral or a printed source.

2. Follow up with a telephone call to be sure that the brochure has been received by the designated project director; use the call to build interest in the firm, learn more about the project, ask for an interview.

3. Use the professional network to find out who else may be competing for the job.

4. Continue to telephone as appropriate.

5. Send along new information (publication tearsheets, reports on new projects begun that might interest this specific client).

6. Keep up the contact until told:

a. The project has been cancelled.

b. Assigned to another firm.

c. The client is totally uninterested.

Chapter Eleven
PREPARING FOR INTERVIEWS

Once your marketing efforts have begun to bring results (or perhaps a referral has come your way), you have an opportunity to rethink the way you handle interviews. As in any performing art, it is what you do *before* the presentation that makes the difference during the performance. The analogy with theater is especially apt. You are the playwright, the director, *and* the actor. By carefully researching the prospective clients' expectations ahead of time and shaping your presentation to them, you offer a "play" that cannot help but capture their attention. By rehearsing yourself beforehand, you can be confident the "script" will be delivered flawlessly by everyone in your "company." Finally, for designers who constantly struggle with stage fright, a little coaching by a speech expert can pay off at the "box office."

LEARNING ABOUT YOUR PROSPECTS

The prospect of an interview can be exciting. Instead of letting the mind race ahead to contemplate what you'll do when you get the job, be smart and put that energy into finding out as much about the prospective client and project as possible. There are several ways this investigation can help you during the interview itself.

Since many designers seem anxious to become more selective about the clients they accept, this is the place to begin. It is the time to research the prospect's history with other designers, including how promptly bills get paid. While you are at it, you can also learn something of the potential client's standards of quality in the area for which you might be hired. This is where a strong niche in your professional network is valuable: Many times you can call another designer out of the blue through a mutual friend and get a totally candid appraisal of the prospect based on prior experience. Even if you are told relatively little you can still learn a lot. But be careful—that person may beat you out of the job if he or she is still on good terms with the prospect!

Several reasons for seeking prior information on the prospects' plans are listed in the accompanying box. All these contribute to making you seem sympathetic to the clients' concerns and thus interested in the job. UDA Architects offer an example: In its role as urban designers, the firm often gathers public but relatively obscure information about a project that is not readily available to another architectural firm seeking

> ### Prior Information on Prospects' Plans Helps You
>
> **To make** your presentation relevant to the clients' needs.
>
> **To be able to ask** productive questions during the interview.
>
> **To be able to intelligently answer** questions the prospect may ask.
>
> **To understand** ahead of time what this job means to the client.

a specific commission within that larger urban development. Using newspapers, maps, public records, and interviews, the Pittsburgh firm makes a preliminary analysis of the planning needs of the city or neighborhood in question and documents the urban context. "The process includes social and financial research with emphasis on human resources," says David Lewis. "Then we translate these findings into visuals: graphics specially prepared for that interview and photographs of the built environment. That helps us make the interviews as personal, direct and human as possible."

Ken Arutunian mentions another motive for careful preparation: "We have found that the level and quality of promotion by our competitors for landscape architecture jobs has improved substantially in recent years. To compete for the 'quality projects,' we have had to improve our proposals as well." AKA, incidentally, spends almost all its marketing time and money preparing for specific project interviews as opposed to general promoting.

Then there is information about how the commission will be awarded. "Questions we ask," says Warren Infield, "are these: Is the client serious or just shopping for price? Will the job be awarded on the designer's reputation? talent? past accomplishments? personality? or just lowest bid? Does the client recognize quality? Can they pay for it?"

SELECTING WORK
TO PRESENT

BASED ON WHAT you have learned about the clients' intentions, you then determine the theme of the message that you want to present at the interview. Although your formal statement should be brief in most cases, its content is important. Select material that focuses on the two or three main points you intend to make, for example, your firm's background in the field, your record of meeting budgets, your history of repeat clients or whatever else will capture the prospects' attention. Use it to reinforce the image of your ability to help them solve their problems through design.

"After we have determined the facts about a potential project such as a psychiatric facility (size, scope of services required, budget information, time frame, and selection criteria)," says Gail Biddison, "we select a few appropriate items (slides, photos, and/or presentation boards) related to the specific job. Overkill turns the client off. Basically we address ourselves to our client's concerns for his specific project and speak to our ability to be helpful to him."

Ed Mills is a bit more specific: "If we are interviewing for an office building, we make up a portfolio of tearsheets and choose slides displaying the office buildings we have worked on in this firm or in previous offices as well as some of the office interiors we have done. We try to make each interview special so that the client doesn't think they are getting standardized treatment."

The point to remember in each of these descriptions is that the choices are made very carefully, avoiding duplication and overemphasis of your specialty. If you have trouble knowing how to limit your selections, ask a business acquaintance who attends such presentations as a buyer to give you a critique before your next presentation. What you may discover is that you are overstating your case. Given our interest in the design process, it's easy to forget that it is the product that the client is interested in. Thus elaborate discourse on how you do the job could actually cost you a commission. Yes, it is important to show how the client's needs are answered but that can be better done perhaps in the question-and-answer portion of the interview.

Information Sources for Specific Projects

Potential clients are the best source of information about their own plans. Approach them directly for help in researching the projects they propose.

Request annual reports and other published materials on the clients' operations.

Consult Dun and Bradstreet's reference books (try local libraries) or other financial sources.

Visit the site or location of the project and discuss the relevant technical issues with the clients' operational personnel.

Study similar facilities or products by the prospect or their competitors.

Read trade publications in the prospects' fields.

Use the telephone and talk to everyone you can who knows how the prospect does business.

Gordon Perry does have a point, however, that may seem a bit contradictory to the foregoing: "I balance out my tailored presentation to show that I am capable of handling many different kinds of products. Sometimes when I'm interviewing somebody who makes medical products and I show some consumer designs, it turns out he or his brother-in-law is also looking for a person to do some consumer work." It never hurts to convey an impression of versatility.

Even if it pays to offer a variety of design examples in your presentation, that doesn't invalidate the cardinal rule here: Less is more. Since the risk of losing a job by boring or overwhelming the prospective client is such a serious possibility for a designer, it is well worth a firmwide effort to streamline and simplify your standard presentation techniques. For instance, any presentation with more than twenty images (or twenty pages with multiple images if you use a portfolio) is likely to be seen—especially where a number of firms are being interviewed—as too much by impatient members of the review committee.

REHEARSING
THE PRESENTATION

KEEPING IN MIND that your presentation is likely a less important part of the interview than the dialogue on client needs, plan to keep its length to one-third maximum of the time allotted for your firm. Since one slide per minute is a good working equation for the number of images to be shown, that makes twenty slides just about right for an hour-long interview. That allows for a

Interior designers (in this case, Will Ching) have found that materials boards from earlier projects can be an effective selling tool during interviews with prospective clients.

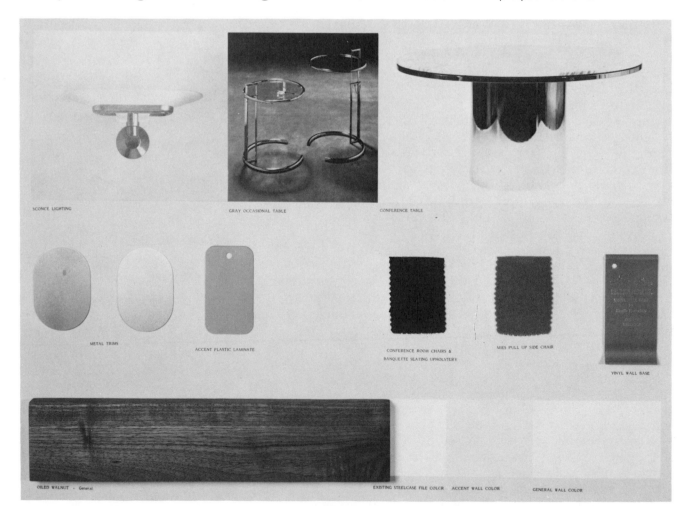

SCONCE LIGHTING   GRAY OCCASIONAL TABLE   CONFERENCE TABLE

METAL TRIMS   ACCENT PLASTIC LAMINATE   CONFERENCE ROOM CHAIRS & BANQUETTE SEATING UPHOLSTERY   MIES PULL UP SIDE CHAIR   VINYL WALL BASE

OILED WALNUT - General   EXISTING STEELCASE FILE COLOR   ACCENT WALL COLOR   GENERAL WALL COLOR

short introduction before the slides and a brief summation afterwards. Refer to page 132 for more on slide presentations.

Then go over the facts that you have gathered on the project and how you intend to respond to them until you know them cold. That frees your mind to pay attention to questions that will be asked and to concentrate on reaching out to the audience. Put the two or three points you want to emphasize on *one* small card. No one minds seeing you refer to a single card; it's when a speaker starts shuffling through a deck of them that audiences get apprehensive.

De Vido suggests that everyone who will be going to the interview should be included in a rehearsal (even if it's done in the car on the way). Home video equipment is no longer exotic or expensive. It offers your firm the opportunity to rehearse important presentations beforehand and see the results. The fun of appearing on camera may well also persuade individuals to participate who might otherwise balk at rehearsing.

Call on everyone you bring to speak, so that the prospects appreciate the depth of your resources. It is also in everyone's interest to have all speeches concise and focused, so you are sure there will be time for questions. But even with critiques by participating associates, sometimes one of your speakers will still run off at the mouth until everyone is embarrassed. That's why it's good to take a tape recorder along. It should help any culprit recognize the problem.

OVERCOMING SHYNESS

THE MAJOR CAUSE for public speakers to ramble on, hem and haw, or repeat themselves is shyness. Instead of stating the facts and sitting down, the uncomfortable speaker tends to prolong the agony for everyone. Bill Koster relates: "The pain of making myself over—conquering shyness—can't be measured in dollars. I was the kind who always threw up before speaking publicly so you can imagine the effort. It's not much of a problem anymore although I'll admit I go into a 'blue funk' the day before interviews even now!" If you have this problem, review the points in the accompanying box.

The jury system in architecture and interior design schools gives many designers a head start on presenting ideas to a potentially hostile audience. If that wasn't enough for you or if you didn't have the opportunity to master your fears in school, don't wait until your next interview to worry about it. For no more than a few hundred dollars you can begin to put that torture behind you.

Ways to Practice Public Speaking

Take a course in public speaking at the community college.

Enroll in a "Dale Carnegie" course.

Join Toastmasters International, a club dedicated to improved public speaking.

Get help from a professional speech consultant.

Volunteer to teach Sunday school.

Practice reading funny stories for an audio or videotape recorder.

Chapter Twelve
INTERVIEWING

THE SECRET OF successful project interviewing is to seduce prospective clients into sharing their hopes and dreams with you, to draw out their emotional expectations. Some designers do that through a natural empathy. For the rest of us the gift of "charm" can be mastered just the way any other behavioral trait is modified or gained. First you have to *want* to change your normal response. Second with the help of a professional, or perhaps just a patient friend, practice asking questions, listening creatively, and putting yourself in the other person's place. Without criticizing the design professions as a whole, it is possible to raise the issue of "arrogance" in *some* designers and to show that it can be very costly at the point when few can afford to pay the price: during the initial interview. The greatest marketing program ever devised can't overcome that liability.

LISTEN AND
ASK QUESTIONS

ACCORDING TO Ann Boyar: "Don't sell yourself. Let a prospective client buy you because you can supply their needs. *Listen* to them and learn what their needs are and then indicate your ability to fulfill them."

"I always put myself in the position of the client," says Pamela Waters. "I listen to him and try to solve not just the problem he brought to me but four others at the same time. Since I understand real estate—maintenance, operations, and management—I can feed my design solution in so I help him in all those areas. That's how I gain his confidence."

Jim Mitchell tells how they do it: "At the initial interview our normal approach is to LISTEN to the client rather than to present our credentials. Our basic assumption is that we wouldn't be there if we weren't qualified. Of course we take promotional material and examples of our work (color prints) which we show if that becomes important. But mainly we develop personal contact with the decision maker."

The idea of showing your wares only when asked may seem such a radical notion that you will not be comfortable with it. If so, then at least you might consider restructuring your presentation. Offer it not as a slide lecture—the conventional approach—but as a matrix for eliciting questions. Since the issue is to get the prospects to talk, the answer may be to request a response to each slide as it appears on the screen or to each presentation board as you put it on the easel. Limit yourself to two or three descriptive phrases and then a question related to the prospects. "Here's a conference room we did for a firm of spaghetti merchants. We used wooden doweling to symbolize their product. Have you thought about how you want your conference room to look?" "We like to use neutral blues and grays with bright accent colors. That's similar to your color scheme in the Chicago office, isn't it?"

Believe it or not, it is easier to get people to talk about their own interests than to pay attention to an elaborate "dog-and-pony show" (that expression does a wonderful job of illuminating the pomposity of most slide shows). And it's a lot less expensive too. Furthermore, you have an opportunity through your questions to express sincere interest in the prospect's problems and enthusiasm for solving them. In short, questions, not answers, should be your style during an interview, unless you are specifically asked to present a statement about your firm.

Finally learn to ask your questions "in the client's language," not in the convoluted jargon of design. Let them realize that you've put some effort in preparing for the interview by asking precise questions about their program, their site, their manufacturing process, their advertising approach, or whatever you can find out about ahead of time. Tell them about similar jobs you've handled, but as those solutions relate to their needs, not about abstract concepts or the prizes won. Pay attention, ask questions, let them know you care about their project.

SELLING GOOD DESIGN

IF MARKETING IS the process of identifying business opportunities, then selling is the art of convincing an individual or a group that employment of your services is necessary to their own business success. That is, convincing them that "good design" pays off. You will have interviews where the prospect is fully prepared to hire a designer and others where he or she is not at all certain that designer services are worth their cost. In each case, the interview gives you the chance to "educate" the potential client. That does not mean lecturing but again responding to their needs in a sympathetic, vigorous fashion.

Supposing the more sophisticated client, the need to explain design will be smaller; in that case there is the possibility of beginning the design process during the interview itself. By raising questions based upon your own research into their circumstances, you can discover preferences and desires that, before the client's eyes, begin to take visual shape. Some interior designers are able, after a few words from the prospect, to paint a beguiling picture of the proposed space with nothing but verbal images and perhaps a few quick strokes with a magic marker.

It is best that you not draw anything to leave behind. Rather, the idea is to use your facility with a pen to illustrate concepts or ideas about the client's problem that make it seem as though you have begun to design. It is to give an impression of openness and generosity that will convince the prospect that you care about getting the job more than someone else does.

For the first-time design client, that technique may not be enough to make the difference. Gere Kavanaugh, who frequently does product design, suggests that the answer here lies in demonstrating for clients that good design can make money for them. Although it applies as well to other design disciplines, it is not an argument that can be made convincingly without preparation. If you have done similar work before, then be ready to show figures that prove economic effectiveness. If not, use your pre-interview research to develop a hypothetical pro forma statement (income versus expense) based on the client's annual report or other financial data. If you are careful not to make extravagant claims for it, such a chart will persuade them that quality design is a worthwhile investment.

HELPING THE "CHEMISTRY" ALONG

SEVERAL DESIGNERS —Pamela Waters, Gail Biddison, Gere Kavanaugh, and Ralph Appelbaum—say that they can feel almost immediately whether a potential client is right for their firm or not. Each claims to have learned the hard way that when the "chemistry" is missing, the project is, if not doomed, then likely to result in emotional difficulties.

It is easy enough to say that a wise designer will pay attention to bad vibrations and avoid such jobs. But what about the cases where things feel a bit strange during the interview, but for other reasons you would like to do the job anyway. The answer lies in trying to find out why the prospect is behaving in a way that makes you uncomfortable. The bold approach is to ask straight out: "What is it about our presentation that you don't like?" A more conservative technique is to frame questions that draw out the other person's feelings rather than factual answers. It may be that your personal style or your work does not appeal to the individual and you are best off knowing that. But chances are that external matters, such as doubts about the project itself or its cost, are causing the awkward response. In that case, you can help the prospect face them and maybe, in the process, win his or her trust.

Some of us have a smoother delivery than others, with charming little jokes always on the tip of the tongue. Whether this is your gift or not, by adopting a light-hearted, easy-going attitude you can help people who find designers intimidating to relax and enjoy the possibility of working with one. We tend to forget that our high-flown social image and our rather obscure interests combine to make "designers" or "architects" a formidable presence across the interview table.

RESPONDING TO CLIENT "POLITICS"

FOR THOSE OF US who deal with corporate or institutional clients, an especially delicate interviewing situation can arise when the executive with whom we have formerly worked is replaced by someone new. One reason for keeping close touch with former clients is to learn of such changes even before they are consummated. The value of an inside "contact"—someone you can count on for information about the latest developments and what they mean—is immeasurable. There are times, of course, when the new vice-president for product development has a favorite design firm he or she wants to bring in, and there is almost nothing you can do about it. Nonetheless, it is important that you approach the new person seriously, offer your services, and try to find out what the policy changes are likely to be. Don't burn bridges that took a long time to build or fail to present yourself for further consideration at such a time.

COMPETING WITH YOUR PEERS

IN EVERY FIELD of design today, competitive interviews have become the norm. Once again, research is a key to success.

As Judith Chafee points out: "My policy is to find out the names of the competing firms. Then I can anticipate the kind of presentation they will give and what points they will stress. I then try to take a different approach to the subject. By removing opportunities for direct comparison, I hope to make the choice cleaner."

Ed Mills notes: "We handle the interview no differently if other firms are competing. If we know any of the competitors, we say complimentary things about them if we say anything at all, since we believe it is important to never criticize other architects publicly."

In graphic and product design, the pace of competition is even more intense than in those disciplines with larger-scope assignments, such as architecture. Those designers have two challenges: First the number of proposals and estimates that must be prepared is greater in order to keep enough jobs coming into the office. Second the prospects often look at designers as suppliers so that price takes precedence over quality. These are also fields in which a design proposal is sometimes expected before the contract is signed or a retainer tendered "on spec."

Even if a fee is promised for visual "ideas," the constant effort of writing proposals and furnishing estimates for the cost of providing service and product is extremely taxing for a small firm. However, Infield + D'Astolfo has found the discipline valuable in the long run. It has forced them to sharpen their proposals and to define their own image more precisely. To differentiate themselves from their competitors, they have learned to speak the clients' language. They tell prospects that the principals will be doing the work, not a staff member the prospect never met.

GETTING "A FOOT IN THE DOOR"

SOMETIMES an interview makes it obvious that the client does not yet know what he or she (or they) want. Either they have not thought out their needs and goals—or factors beyond their control have not been adequately researched. In any case a final decision on choosing the designer will be postponed. That is when the clever professional will propose doing a study that will clarify the issues. Perhaps the client will have thought of sponsoring research before the meeting, but it is in the nature of design training that we can think complex problems through right before their eyes—and create a job for ourselves during the interview.

Jeanne Hartnett has made "feasibility studies capability" an important part of her marketing approach. For a fixed fee, her firm offers to do that type of work on the expectation that "if we perform satisfactorily they will wish to proceed with the balance of the work; if they do not go ahead, we help them see that they have risked minimum dollars on that one phase."

Ralph Appelbaum has developed his own approach to convincing potential clients of his firm's value. For museums and institutions distant from his New York City office, he offers one- or two-day paid "consultancies" during which he helps them figure out their problem. By "figure out," Ralph means that he will apply his particular discipline to it; he shows the client what they must do, how his firm could fit in, and

---

Questions to Ask BEFORE the Interview

Research

Who is the client representative? Who is the decision-maker?

Who else is on the interview committee?

What are the client needs?

What is the project scope and budget?

Who else is competing?

Preparation

How much time for the interview?

What are the facilities in the interview room?

How do the client's needs relate to our firm's experience and specialties?

How do we best convey our firm's diversity?

What kind of "show" is best in this case?

When do we rehearse?

Presentation

Who will be the spokesperson for our firm?

How will the others participate?

Who will take notes or operate the taperecorder?

Do we need to prepare a prospect question list in advance?

How do we shut off a long-winded colleague?

How can we be sure we *listen* to the client?

Why are we going to this interview anyway?

where the process will take them. And after he has briefed himself on the project this way, he can make "a more intimate pitch" for the work. Recently after two days on one such consultancy in the southwest, he was asked to take on the project.

SCARING
PROSPECTS AWAY

As WITH ANY of the elite, educated professions today, designers tend to believe that the world revolves around their discipline. They are encouraged to focus on it single-mindedly in school, to look up to the "stars" who are adulated in professional journals, and to seek out peers for social companionship.

This narrow focus leads designers to expect that everybody else will care about their esthetic perceptions and understand their jargon and that clients will be happy to see their work from the point of view of "design." Not only are all these notions false, but pursuit of them is almost guaranteed to cost you potential commissions and, even if you get a few jobs, to cause endless communication difficulties. Remember, practicing design is a business, not an elegant hobby. Learn to see things from your clients' standpoint, not the other way around.

Chapter Thirteen
WHAT TO DO
AFTER THE INTERVIEW

MANY DESIGNERS, including people who participated in this book, do not send a letter or otherwise communicate with the individuals whom they have just interviewed. Their attitude seems to be that any overt action on the designer's part will appear "pushy" and will offend the prospect. So they sit by the telephone and wait. More times than not, the person interviewed never calls to offer the job, and perhaps, even worse, the timid designer never finds out why.

Just as follow-up is a crucial ingredient in the early stages of marketing, it can make the difference here between getting the job and losing it—feeling you've wasted your energy at an interview one more time. If you accept the premise that a designer ought to go after work, then a strong response after an interview should seem as logical as going to the meeting itself. It shows you truly want the job.

REITERATING
CLIENT NEEDS

A PLEASANT NOTE thanking the interview committee for its attention is better than no letter at all. But a letter that also reviews the issues discussed during the meeting has two advantages: First it records in a concise way the content of the interview (which can be helpful to the interviewers themselves); and second it gives you an opportunity to comment on the items as you report them.

"After the interview," says Bill Koster, "we send a letter strengthening points we made (or covering those we missed). Sometimes we send a different letter to each interviewer on the committee appealing to his or her special interest as expressed in questions or responses during the meeting. We have learned that often they compare these letters and in that way get a broader understanding of our firm."

Obviously that kind of response calls for a great deal of sensitivity during the interview itself, very good notes or a tape that can be analyzed later, as well as enough time spent composing and typing each letter. Yet it seems inexpensive if it sways an uncertain committee in your direction. Keep in mind that a group of people who intend to hire a designer will probably spend at least as much time talking about it together later as they did in the interview themselves. Any way that you can put your firm forward during those discussions is fair game. If you have a "supporter" on the committee, that will no doubt help your case. Be sure to furnish him or her with a good set of notes based on your response to the interview so that any points you thought of afterward can be aired.

Assuming however that you have no such advantage, the follow-up letter should be a reportlike statement of two or three pages. Each concern raised during the interview is listed with a short statement of how your firm will specifically address it. This varies from one discipline to another, but in most cases it is appropriate to include design ideas about the project in the letter. Diagrams that may have been sketched in the meeting can be cleaned up a bit; relationships between parts of the project can be illustrated; emphasizes and proportions that you would suggest may be included. Everything short of actually revealing your design solution can be useful in the letter. Even revealing the design, if the interview was with a former client or if your field of design customarily offers sketches before agreements are finalized (as is the case in advertising design), may make sense in your case. A follow-up letter, however, is not the same as a proposal to do the job, and thus such elaborate documentation may be premature or out of order.

DRAFTING PROPOSALS

THERE ARE TWO principal distinctions between a follow-up letter and a proposal: First the prospective client must request that you submit a proposal before you do so. Second you definitely include a quotation of the fee you will charge in the proposal (not necessarily the case with a follow-up letter).

There are four elements in the normal proposal: (1) statement of your firm's qualifications, including prior business experience if appropriate; (2) your understanding of the scope of the project, including tentative budget; (3) management process you will follow, including tentative schedule; and (4) fee statement. These elements need not necessarily be done in that order. Some designers prefer to place their statement of how they understand the nature and scope of the project right up front, leaving the qualification data and personnel resumes near the end.

Ed Mills finds that it takes his firm anywhere from one to ten hours to prepare proposals, perhaps expedited by a standard format that his firm has evolved over the past 4½ years of practice. Other offices say that it takes considerably longer: Jim Mitchell tries to put off the proposal until several meetings after the initial interviews have been held. There are two advantages: You will have learned so much more about the client needs that the statement can be shorter and simpler than if you must speculate on their goals; also you are more certain that the job is likely to come your way.

Institutional clients usually demand a complete statement as part of the designer selection process. If you make the shortlist, a formal proposal is required. Ken Arutunian's landscape design firm has developed an in-house method for preparing them that delivers a booklet designed to compete with the proposals of large northern California landscape architecture "corporations." These can take "several days of preparation." For example, for the renovation of an existing university amphitheater, AKA submitted a forty-page brochure that included the following material:

☐ Under qualifications, a general statement of the firm's history and short resumes of the professional staff.

☐ For scope of project, a short essay on "Project Understanding" and ten photographs of the site, with captions stating the problems that the firm has identified with suggested solutions.

☐ Work or management process includes a step-by-step statement of the project design and planned documentation drawings followed by a fold-out flow chart that covers all phases and client consultation meetings.

☐ Finally, after a selection of ten related jobs they've completed (two pages for each), a project construction schedule and a list of hourly rates for staff and consultants.

UDA Architects also use graphic means to document their proposals: "We put our projects on a flow chart which shows who does what and when. This in turn can be broken out into projections of per diems, travel, subsistence, and other costs, etc., all of which become useful tools in negotiating the fee, since they create a climate of professional competence and accountability which assists in closing the deal."

No matter what, keep your writing simple—short words, short sentences, and short on jargon. (See accompanying box for a proposal checklist.)

> *Proposal Checklist*
>
> **Statement of qualifications**
>   Project personnel resumes
>   Consultant resumes
>   Examples of completed
>   work
>
> **Understanding of project scope**
>
> **Description of management process**
>   Documentation and
>   production process
>   Project completion schedule
>
> **Fee statement**

QUOTING FEES

KEN ARUTUNIAN recommends: "Spend enough research time to be able to present a well thought-out fee proposal. In the past, a firm may have been selected and then a fee negotiated; now fee is an important factor itself in the selection of design services. One must be competitive no matter how qualified he or she may be for a particular project."

To the client the single most interesting part of your proposal is what your work will cost. A proposal without it will not be taken seriously. Ambiguous or overly complicated schedules for remuneration are likely to be interpreted as incompetence on your part, even though you may see them as options that can save the prospective client money.

The fee statement should be as straightforward as the rest of the proposal. Put down the method and amount that you want for the work you are offering to do: for example, "We will furnish design and production drawings for a wooden folding chair in return for (a) an advance payment of $1,800 (half due upon signing contract and the remainder due upon delivery of technical drawings); and (b) a five percent (5n) royalty on each unit sold." Even if you are prepared to negotiate, don't say so in writing. There is usually an opportunity to let the right person know informally that you are prepared to discuss it.

GETTING FEEDBACK
(IF YOU DON'T GET THE JOB)

YOU CAME OUT of the interview feeling that you had them eating out of your hand, right? Nonetheless, the form letter comes in a few days saying that while the committee was very impressed by your qualifications, another firm was awarded the contract.

Yes, it is the hardest thing in the world to pick up the telephone to find out why you didn't get the job. Will Ching is one person who has gotten over that hump by realizing that feedback from those he had hoped to serve is the most valuable resource he can salvage from a disaster.

Make it easy by calling the person on the committee whom you know best or whom you felt was most supportive of your presentation. Wait to call until you have gotten over the worst of the depression, and make sure not to complain or sound downhearted. Then, instead of blurting out, "What did we do wrong?" ask why the winner was chosen. Any reasonably sympathetic person on the other end of the line will get around to filling you in on why you lost without assaulting you. Always ask if fees had anything to do with it. You may not want to offer to discuss lowering your price, but Ching has taught himself to grit his teeth and make the offer. Sometimes, he says, "What had been an enthusiastic response to my services is killed by a hastily considered bid. I sharpen my pencil and get back to them."

Remember that even this kind of contact has marketing value. Now they know something about your work and will probably be happy to assuage guilt feelings by inviting you back for a future interview. Put the person whom you have called on your list for general twice-a-year mailings or newsletter. And keep in touch. "Timing is critical," says Gordon Perry. "If you don't follow up as you should, someone else will be calling on the prospective client. When your opportunity comes up, the person who is on the spot will get the job."

LOOKING IN ON
THE JOB LATER

ANOTHER KIND of follow-up on a successful "sale" that Pamela Waters has turned to marketing advantage is to go a year or so after it is complete to check out how the installation is working out. Then she writes the owner a short but constructive letter with suggestions for updating certain elements, replacing defective parts or upgrading maintenance. She sees it as one more way to let your client know that you care about more than just getting paid for your designs. It is also a great opportunity, she notes, to propose a lunch "so you can each catch up on the other's latest project."

In summary, follow-up can take a hundred different forms. Think of it as keeping the ball rolling once you've thrown it toward a potential business partner. You never know when a routine telephone call or attractive mailing item will coincide with an unexpected need for design services. If the mailing never goes out or if the call gets put off indefinitely, the likelihood of such serendipitous surprises is mighty small.

Chapter Fourteen
CLOSING THE DEAL

THE PROCESS you use in promoting and selling a design project shapes the final result. This includes the type of agreement that you sign with the client. For example, a businesslike approach at contract-signing time impresses clients since they are usually business people themselves.

SETTING FEES

THERE ARE MANY different ways to get paid for your work. Some methods, like the hourly rate, apply at times to any design field. Others, like a percentage of the cost of construction or royalties, relate to architecture or product design, respectively. A substantial list of alternatives follows, many of which offer distinct advantages to the designer (see page 118).

But from the standpoint of marketing, one type of fee offers advantages over all the rest: the lump sum or fixed price for services. Clients have always had trouble understanding why design costs so much. The two reasons why design/build companies in the commercial building field have been successful are that design services appear to be thrown in at no extra cost and because a fixed-price contract is offered for the whole job. Everyone likes a fixed price when buying dinner or a suit of clothes. When, to the client, the budget involves seemingly astronomical sums of money, the desire for predictable costs naturally multiplies as well. Thus, even if you can't control the production cost of a job, the most attractive design fee proposal you can offer is the lump sum.

Despite the risks, a well-organized firm (or one thoroughly experienced in the sort of project under consideration) can safely offer a fixed-price contract for design services. Effective cost-accounting procedures pursued for at least two or three years should enable you to accurately predict the number of hours needed for a job. Multiply them by the appropriate hourly rates and add overhead and profit (about 20 percent). Then include a contingency factor to cover those unpredictable elements that make the hourly rate so attractive. If you are rather sure of your figures and the job is straightforward, 10 percent will probably suffice. If you have doubts about your costs or about the client's intentions, add 25 to 100 percent. The important thing is to offer a total number of dollars. In return for the certainty of a fixed price, the client is paying a premium to hold your attention until the job is completed.

Type of Fees

	Name	When Applicable	Special
1.	Lump sum of fixed fee	General use, separately and as part of a total project cost (graphic design)	Very attractive to clients, but great care is needed to anticipate and control change in project scope and required services.
2.	Hourly	General use	Actual costs must be multiplied by 2.5 or 3 in order to be profitable.
3.	Cost plus a fee	General use	Requires thorough accounting but may be the fairest method to all parties. Fee can be fixed or a percentage of total costs.
4.	Percentage of project cost	Primarily new building design	Use a multiphase contract that calls for 85 to 90% of fee paid by completion of contract document phase—remainder should be profit.
5.	Fee per square foot	Space planning/ interior design	For repetitive planning only. Use hourly rate for more elaborately designed areas.
6.	Retail	Residential interior design	Traditional with some interior designers who buy at wholesale and include design services in retail price to client. Often unprofitable.
7.	Royalties	Product design and publishing	Represents speculation by designer or writer. May not be profitable. An investment rather than a fee.
8.	Part ownership	Real estate development	Fee taken as stock in a speculative venture: An investment rather than a fee.
9.	Retainership	Primarily product design	Annual agreement putting design services at first call of client. Should be in addition to an hourly rate.
10.	Fee determined by type of use	Graphic design	Agreement based on national versus local exposure, four-color, single-color, categories of advertising and promotional functions.
11.	Fee for reuse and extended use	Graphic design	Most contracts are for one-time use only: This clause covers additional fees for multiple use.
12.	Work for hire	Graphic design	Caution is advised; by signing such a contract, designer or illustrator surrenders all copyrights to the buyer.

Each design discipline has its favorite way to charge for services. But for a firm with good control of its production costs, the lump sum or fixed fee has definite marketing advantages.

NEGOTIATING

SOMETIMES, when you've done a spectacular job at the interview but the committee feels your price is a bit too high, they'll ask you to consider some sort of an adjustment. If you also liked them, there may be a legitimate opportunity for bargaining. One possibility is to offer two or three different ways to bill for your services as Gordon Perry does. When he is talking to a product manufacturer, for instance, he will suggest: (1) a fixed fee payable in stages, (2) a 3 to 5 percent royalty on each unit sold, or (3) an hourly rate structure. Depending on the amount of capital the prospect can put into design, the deal is made.

To help clients unfamiliar with the phased method of billing used by interior designers and architects (or any other way a fee is calculated), it is useful to explain how the work is carried out so that the charges begin to make sense. Jordan/Mitchell uses its microcomputer to print out fee breakdowns that not only explain the number of hours to be spent on each phase for each category of expense but that take 20 percent for profit and contingency right off the top.

Here is where profitability becomes a big issue. The key, in Ralph Appelbaum's experience, is to know where the line between profitability and loss lies in a particular fee proposal. If you know where that limit is, you can negotiate in an authoritative fashion. The client, especially a person who knows business, will respect your explanation of design process costs—including profit—if you convince them you are not padding your fee unreasonably. Negotiation, of course, is a two-way street. If the client can't afford full services, you can always offer to do less—lower the scope of the project—assuming a satisfactory job is still possible.

A hint—small but important. Be sure your agreement allows you to photograph and publicize the completed project. There is always the chance of rough sledding during the project, and you want to ensure the client's cooperation after it is over.

GET THEM TO SIGN

SALESPEOPLE ARE taught to fill out the form while discussing the sale with the customer, to total the price and then offer a pen for the signature. Don't give 'em time to think it over!

For designers the contract process is more complicated, but the need to press for a commitment is no less an issue. That's why, whether you use standard contract documents or a letter of agreement, be prompt and politely assertive in presenting it to your client.

Even the most battle-worn designers are tempted to begin work on a new project before the contract has been signed. Don't. And furthermore, insist on a retainer. Gere Kavanaugh says: "I learned the hard way not to start a job without a retainer. They only mean business if they come across with that advance payment!" The size of the retainer is a matter of personal choice. There are interior designers, for example, who ask $1,000 no matter how large the job, and there are those who ask for one-third to one-half of the total fee up front—and get it!

SELLING TOO HARD

JUDITH CHAFEE says: "Warning: Do not become so involved in the goal of selling that you sell yourself into a relationship that will not be rewarding personally and/or financially. Look at potential clients with care. Relax enough to really listen to them and decide whether the tenor of their responses might hint at future trouble. There is always *another* prospect out there."

Does "discount design" ever pay? It is not anyone else's business if a designer chooses to work for fees that are significantly lower than the standard in his or her field. It is one way to get started in practice. Ralph Appelbaum calls it the "Theory of Accommodation": "At first a designer follows small carrots on very long poles. Later, as one's time becomes more billable, one realizes he can restrain his generosity and still hold clients. I don't take the low-budget jobs I did at first, but the credits gained were valuable enough to justify the investment of energy."

Who can say that working for lower-than-normal fees is wrong? What does appear to be true is that practicing design on an unprofitable basis for more than a year or two can be emotionally debilitating, to say nothing of its economic consequences. Marketing can help you avoid the problem and is, therefore, an integral part of a healthy design practice.

Things to Do	*Things to Avoid*
Practice using the telephone for marketing and selling.	**Haphazard** once-in-a-while mailing programs.
Structure your calling technique to gather as much information as possible, even though the prospect may not be interested in seeing you.	**Designer jargon** and talk about "process" to prospects.
	Complicated, over-long presentations of your work.
Identify and seek out the decision-makers in organizations that you would like to work for.	**Bad-mouthing** the competition during interviews.
	Unclear statements about how you want to be paid.
Follow up persistently on prospects that your marketing uncovers.	**Assuming** that your prospects always pay their bills without running a credit check.
Take suppliers and contractors to lunch and ask about potential projects they may know of.	**Beginning work** without a signed contract or a retainer.
	Jobs that demand more time than they are worth in fees or future possibilities (always think carefully before giving too much away in the latter category).
Research the client's needs before the interview.	
Listen and ask questions during the interview.	
If you don't get the job, call up and find out why you didn't.	

UDA Architects

249 N. Craig Street,
Pittsburgh, Pennsylvania 15213-1592
Architecture, urban design, planning

Established: 1964

Staff (1983): Four principals, five senior associates, five junior associates, two designers, two administrative staff

Educational Background:
David Lewis, FAIA:
Diploma of Architecture,
Leeds University (U.K.);
Raymond L. Gindroz:
B.Arch., M.Arch. (urban design),
Carnegie-Mellon University;
James P. Goldman: B.Arch.,
Carnegie-Mellon University;
Donald K. Carter: B. Arch.,
Carnegie-Mellon University, Graduate Studies in Urban Design and Planning at Edinborough University (U.K.) and Harvard University

Teaching Positions:
Lewis and Gindroz: Carnegie-Mellon University;
Gindroz: Yale University

Professional Societies:
American Institute of Architects (Carter, President of Pittsburgh Chapter);
Royal Institute of British Architects (RIBA),
American Institute of Certified Planners (AICP),
American Planning Association (AAP)

Photos: © Stan Franzos

David Lewis

Raymond L. Gindroz

James P. Goldman

Donald K. Carter

PROFESSIONAL FRAMEWORK.
Focused around urban design, the four architect partners of UDA have diverse but interrelated interests. David Lewis, the senior partner, is known internationally for his contribution on the emerging profession of urbanism. Ray Gindroz, partner in charge of design, spends time each year (as does Lewis) teaching urban design. Jim Goldman gets the firm's projects built, and Donald Carter is expanding their activities into real estate development. The firm encourages community participation in almost every urban design or planning project they undertake. The office is organized as a workshop in which teams follow a project all the way through, managed by a senior staff project architect. This group is augmented by staff specialists as the work progresses.

GOALS AND OBJECTIVES. Specialization in urban design is UDA's primary marketing direction. In their case, it has meant defining the market at the same time the office has been seeking work in it. "Our first marketing efforts concentrated on differentiating our urban design-oriented approach to architecture," says David Lewis. Half of his professional time is charged to marketing the firm's expertise through preparation of scholarly articles, leadership of seminars for municipal governments as well as international urban design conferences, and service on AIA'S Rural/Urban Design Assistance Teams (R/UDAT).

MARKETING STRATEGY. The major promotion effort—David Lewis's lecturing and writing—has been aimed as much at developing the profession of urban design as UDA itself. Yet there is a clear link between his work and the firm's burgeoning fortunes: One large-scale urban design project can generate specific architectural projects—new construction as well as renovation—that will keep an office busy for years. UDA finds that their international reputation helps the firm maintain a strong referral operation in western Pennsylvania. Their folder is full of small-scale urban renovation projects that illustrate a down-to-earth interest in reuse of old buildings with new construction inserted among them that echoes the existing styles. UDA has chosen to operate without a formal marketing plan and without a designated partner in charge of marketing. It is, to them, an extension of their workshop approach to practice. Far from ignoring the problems of marketing, UDA has worked with three separate consultants (page 20) to understand better how to focus their promoting and selling energies.

PROMOTION TACTICS. The partners hold weekly meetings during which they review their list of prospects, discuss the status of each lead, and often come up with new ways of approaching them. The process involves looking for opportunities in their region among planning officials and developers to create private/public partnerships. Combining these two sectors to create new or improved community facilities within an urban context is what UDA does best.

PROMOTION MATERIALS. UDA has developed some low-cost ways to tell people about their work. One of their consultants, graphic designer Diana Riddle, has given them two color-coordinated folders and a credentials brochure for $3,500. Into the smaller of the two folders, they insert, as appropriate, examples from a large series of project description sheets prepared in the office. These include urban design demonstration projects that document the firm's experience as a pioneer in the field. Using homemade line renderings and plans that reproduce well on the office's photocopier, UDA is able to convey a solid impression of their expertise. They also have a substantial set of magazine tearsheets depicting completed projects.

EVALUATION. In its twenty-year existence, marketing has never been seen as a necessity by UDA. The firm's good record of public exposure and well-received community design participation projects have generated enough work to increase its staff to almost twenty people. Promotion through David Lewis's international efforts and a good local record as a competent architectural office have kept the jobs rolling in. Ray Gindroz recognizes that the firm should keep in closer touch with former clients and should follow up more vigorously on project opportunities generated by UDA's completed work. As the office grows, however, the need to reach out will increase. Larger operating expenses will generate cash-flow demands that can only be met through more stuctured business planning and marketing. UDA is on the threshold, in effect, of opportunity. It is internationally known in its specialty, well-thought of locally, and widely published. By reaching out to those whom the partners have identified as desirable potential clients, this firm can use its track record to win better commissions than it now has.

The variety of media created to promote the North Shore Center including a map that relates it to downtown Pittsburgh, illustrates the range of promotional techniques employed by UDA Architects to market their urban design-based architectural services. Typical page from a six-page UDA foldout promotion piece (opposite page) printed on a heavy stock depicts important projects beneath a continuing horizontal line. Space above the line is used to tell client prospects which services UDA offers and how the designer would work with them.

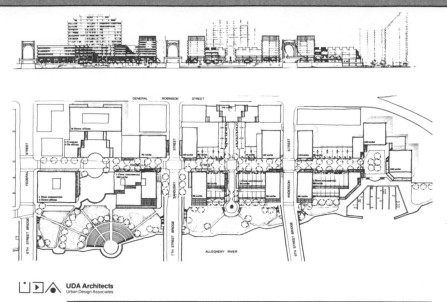

UDA Architects
Urban Design Associates

North Shore Master Plan

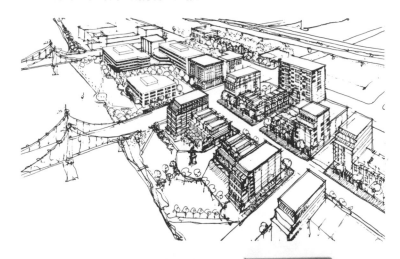

Photo: Lockwood Hoehl

Project Organization

UDA Architects' office is organized as a workshop. Each project is supervised by a Partner-in-Charge and is managed by a senior staff Project Architect. Other partners and specialist staff architects are involved in every project in terms of their particular skills as the work progresses.

Architecture of New Buildings

The project list of UDA Architects includes corporate offices, commercial buildings, hotels, housing, sports facilities, schools, community centers, university buildings, health care facilities, parking structures, and many other building types.

From small buildings to multi-million dollar complexes, in rural locations or high-density urban sites, the range of our award-winning architecture demonstrates our versatility.

Restoration and Adaptive Re-use

We believe that wherever it makes economic sense to do so, old buildings and the historic fabric of our cities should be retained and kept alive.

Our work in conservation includes the recycling of historic buildings and entire Historic Districts, several of which are on the National Register of Historic Places.

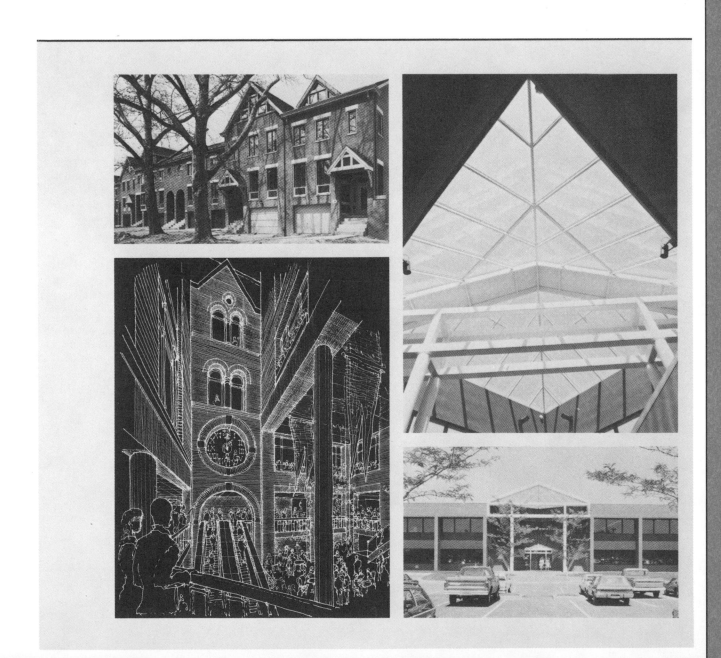

Radford-Biddison

1440 Aldenham Lane,
Reston, Virginia 22090

Contract interior design

Established: 1980

Staff (1983):
Two principals, one professional staff,
one administrative staff

Educational Background:
Pam Radford: B.A. (history), University
of Colorado;
Gail Biddison: Rochester Institute of
Technology; B.A. (interior design),
Mount Vernon College

Professional Societies:
Biddison: American Society of Interior
Designers;
Environmental Design Research
Association (EDRA)

Pam Radford   Gail Biddison

Radford-Biddison's quietly elegant
credentials brochure is complemented
by professional photographs (such as
the Georgetown University Intercultural
Center in McGhee Library shown here)
in the promotional packages they mail.

PROFESSIONAL FRAMEWORK.

When Pam Radford and Gail Biddison decided to join forces, they each brought substantial experience in large-scale contract interiors work to the partnership. Radford had worked on healthcare facilities before setting up and running the interior design department of an international architectural firm's Washington office. Biddison worked with her there, and together they did several long-range planning and programming studies for very large federal and other healthcare and commercial projects. Thus they began their practice prepared for any size job. They also brought an awareness of the importance of marketing to the new business. Pam had managed both a small high-quality interior design office and a large operation associated with the architectural firm. The latter position involved new business development so she had no trouble assuming the same role for the partnership.

GOALS AND OBJECTIVES.

Radford and Biddison realized that their experience in planning and design for hospitals and psychiatric facilities was their primary strength. But they also wanted to branch out into new areas of specialization such as corporate space planning and design. Their goals then were centered around diversity and, at the same time, the market with which they were already familiar. In the latter case, they had to establish themselves as a new pro-

fessional presence with institutions that knew them in another capacity. The partners chose to begin a new practice then at least partly so that they could broaden their experience as designers. At the same time they intended to use their expertise in medical facilities to get their new firm off to a good start.

MARKETING STRATEGY.

Since Radford is the partner in charge of marketing, it has been her duty to keep up with the business publications from which the office draws many of its leads, to make cold calls, to follow up and oversee that part of the business. She spends about one-quarter of her time at it. The partners are aware that much more of her time should be spent on marketing. Biddison's efforts at promotion and selling vary from "nearly 90 percent some weeks to none other times," she says. While they have not found books or seminars on marketing to be especially appropriate for their needs, they are quite enthusiastic about the value of networking with peers: "We compare notes with fellow professionals at every opportunity to see what techniques they have found successful. This can be both provocative and helpful. Their approach may not be exactly applicable, but it stirs up new possibilities and ideas which may work for us."

PROMOTION TACTICS.

Radford-Biddison employs a telephone marketing sequence that contacts prospects whom they find by reviewing publications in their specialties. After the first call, they send their qualifications brochure and a cover letter requesting an interview. In a week, they call to be sure the brochure has been received. Within two weeks they call again to request an interview. After that, they monitor interested but inactive prospects by calling every few weeks to check the status of the project. One of these contacts often leads, they have found, to another through referrals.

PROMOTION MATERIALS.

Pam Radford and Gail Biddison have developed a credentials brochure that they used for the direct mail program already noted. It is a four-page

folder, warm gray, that has nothing but the firm name in silver with green trim on the front cover and its address in drop-out type on the back cover. Inside a carefully lit photograph of the two partners at work is followed by a detailed description of their individual professional experience. The facing page states their services and lists former clients, all in drop-out type on the same gray field. With a graphic consultant, they spent $2,000 on it. The partners have gotten a response they felt justified the expense. They sought a document that would convincingly demonstrate Radford-Biddison's professional commitment. At the same time they wanted to offer prospects a brochure whose formal appearance would encourage the receiver to file it rather than throw it away.

EVALUATION. Two women who have worked in large offices doing enormous space planning projects decided that they want to practice interior design in a more selective fashion. Radford-Biddison have used promotion and selling techniques developed with their former employer to serve the goals that motivated them to form their new practice. They are constantly on the lookout for job opportunities. But they have found, as many small design firms do, that the intent to promote and sell vigorously is often compromised by the need to produce work already on the boards. That dilemma, as these designers recognized, can be softened by setting realistic marketing objectives based on the firm's limited time and resources.

NOTE. In June 1983, the Radford-Biddison partnership was dissolved. "The dissolution represents," says Gail Biddison, "a further progression in the process that began with the partners leaving the large firm in 1980 to practice design in a way which permits both professional growth and personal flexibility."

Voorsanger and Mills Associates, Architects

30 West 57 Street,
New York City 10019

Interior architecture

Established: 1978

Staff (1983): Two principals, one
associate, twelve project architects,
three administrative staff

Educational Background:
Bartholomew Voorsanger: B.A.,
Princeton University,
École des Beaux Arts Fellowship,
Fontainebleau, France,
M.Arch., Harvard University;
Edward I. Mills: B.Arch.,
North Carolina State University,
M.Arch., Harvard University

Teaching Positions:
Both principals: Visiting Professor of
Architecture, Columbia University
(in alternating years)

Professional Society:
American Institute of Architects

Bartholomew Voorsanger
Edward Mills

PROFESSIONAL FRAMEWORK.
After years of training in I. M. Pei's office and others that involved project management responsibilities, Voorsanger and Mills struck out on their own in 1978. The subsequent path of accomplishment has been well documented in the design press. Clearly identified with "post-modernism," Voorsanger and Mills produce designs with elegant detailing soundly based in classical precedent and masterful use of color. Their partnership has had to adjust rapidly to growth pressures due to their success. But the firm stands by its original intention to "commit the principals to direct participation in every job from the early phases of project planning and development through construction supervision." The partners have made a point of promoting their assistants to run jobs as quickly as individual expertise permits. Nonetheless, they supervise these people intensively to maintain a proper balance between design enthusiasm and experience. The partners meet at least monthly with their accountant and office manager to keep track of project schedules and budgets as well as financial matters related to the practice itself.

GOALS AND OBJECTIVES.
At this point, Voorsanger and Mills seek clients whom they feel both want and can afford the elaborate, carefully crafted interiors that the firm can provide. They are also interested in larger projects in order to increase fees and, they hope, profits. In spite of their success with architectural interiors, Voorsanger and Mills intends to pursue a general practice rather than specialize.

MARKETING STRATEGY.
Publication in design magazines is the primary marketing tactic of the firm. Like other designers who have trained in offices with a national reputation, the partners understand the power of a few glossy pages from a magazine to convince potential clients of their credibility. Thus they have cultivated the interest of editors in their projects both by tours that they conduct and professional quality photographs that they provide. Their colorful (both in hue and form) work is particularly effective on the printed page—a characteristic that contributes to the frequency with which they are published.

PROMOTION TACTICS.
A benefit of publication in professional magazines, reported by others profiled in this book as well, is that other architects and designers frequently recommend Voorsanger and Mills to potential clients. In fact they say peers are the best source of work they have. Such referrals fall into three categories: (1) interiors projects that their former employers send to them, (2) New York jobs referred to them by architects located too far away to carry them out efficiently, and (3) out-of-town projects that other large New York offices cannot do economically. Ninety percent of these prospects then call Voorsanger and Mills directly. Everyone who comes knocking at their door wants what the firm has

Peter Aaron/ESTO

Crisply detailed views of a Long Island house (opposite page) and Le Cygne, a Manhattan restaurant (left), are typical of the professional photography that has helped Voorsanger and Mills achieve wide publication and through it a successful practice.

already mastered, while the partners would like to avoid being cast in a specialty mold.

EVALUATION. If they truly wish to develop a diverse practice, then Voorsanger and Mills must go out and find clients for the kinds of work they claim to want, just like any other practice. That is much harder for them to do (since both partners run each job personally) than if the office were hungry for work. Voorsanger and Mills, who admit to

occasional slow periods during which they spend a few hours each week wondering where the next job is coming from, are ideal candidates for a full-fledged marketing program. Where many designers have to figure out how to put their name before the public, they have that well under control. Where most firms have to take about every job that is offered, Voorsanger and Mills can and do refer prospects to other designers. Although inadequate cash flow might

limit their efforts, here is a case where an appropriate marketing director could be extremely effective. Given clear goals and strong direction by the partners, he or she would search for opportunities that suit the firm's goals. Those prospects would become the subject of a well-planned selling campaign. The intended result is larger and more challenging projects than those realized during the firm's early years.

Pamela Waters Studio, Inc.

320 West 13th Street,
New York City 10014

General design consultants specializing in plazas, lobbies, and print graphics

Established: 1969

Staff (1983): Principal, office manager, part-time bookkeeper, vice-president of print graphics; senior designer for 3-D projects; junior designer

Educational Background:
B.I.D., Pratt Institute

Professional Societies:
Industrial Design Society of America; Illuminating Engineering Society (IES); Honorary member, Women in Design; President, Friends of Hanover Square (NYC)

Pamela Waters

PROFESSIONAL FRAMEWORK.
Pamela Waters intends her lobby-and-plaza designs for Manhattan office buildings to surprise and amuse passersby. "I want to do permanent things—not exhibits—that affect the community I live in," she says. "I obviously have the right skills because what I've done gets lots of response and I get more work from it. In fact, the visibility of my projects is the key to my success in business." By her own choice, Waters keeps the office small. She does it to guarantee her personal involvement in each project. With three or four assistants at most, Waters feels she can be more selective about her projects than if she supported a bigger staff.

Another basis for her freedom is a strong referral connection with some of Manhattan's major commercial real-estate owners. It was her collaboration with one of the most colorful of these developer/owners, Mel Kaufman, that began her practice. His lower Manhattan office tower at 127 John Street, which included her work in its vivid collection of design elements, launched Pamela Waters as an original spirit in the world of design.

GOALS AND OBJECTIVES. The strongest goal for her practice then is to preserve its variety and diversity. She calls her business "Pamela Waters Studio" to express that atelierlike point of view. Along with her obvious design talents, Waters has a good head for business. "My accountants tell me I have impeccable business sense. I don't know why but I just know how to deal with people. That's why I like working directly with owner/builders, the ones actually doing the work." Through her work on commercial building lobbies and streetscape design, she has branched out into print graphics. "When I see a client using a typeface on a flier that is not suitable for the sign on his building, good professional manners require that I tell him it should be coordinated. I don't care if I do it or some other guy does. My contribution professionally is to bring it up—maybe the client never thought of it. His

Unexpected visual delight in her designs for Manhattan office building lobbies (747 Third Avenue shown above) and plazas (767 Third Avenue shown on page 130) have won acclaim and clients for Pamela Waters.

confidence in me is then enhanced." Her work in print graphics began when she suggested to the owner/builders that their stationery and marketing literature ought to be upgraded to match the style of her design. By promoting skills to these clients that are a natural extension of what she was already doing for them, Waters has broadened her business.

MARKETING STRATEGY. She makes a conscious effort to keep in touch with her owner/builder clients as noted elsewhere. News of her latest project quickly gets around to other Manhattan landlords. They can go judge for themselves how effective it is. Waters often gets calls from building owners who have already checked her out with former clients. Sometimes her first meeting with the prospect is in the lobby she is

being asked to redesign. In other words, the project is awarded even before she gets to show her slideshow. When one of this community of owners does a nice job on a project that *didn't* involve her services, Waters will drop him a congratulatory note anyway. "Marketing is just good professional manners," she says.

PROMOTION TACTICS. "If I don't have a response to a potential client that I'm going to click with him (and you can't click with everybody), I don't take the job. I know by instinct whether we'll get anywhere, whether we'll have fun with the project. Otherwise no dice. If you do what you like best and you like the person you're working with, you'll have profitability and all those other business things. It also means you don't

have trouble getting paid. They all go hand in hand." Waters has no printed material describing her practice. When a prospect requests information, she stuffs a few magazine tearsheets into a manila envelope and sends it with a request that it be returned when that person is finished with it.

EVALUATION. Pamela Waters has learned to capitalize on flamboyance that laypeople often expect from designers. Her promotion and selling style is of a piece with her design esthetic, and that may be why it works so well for her. She is good at selling face to face because she is able to transmit her enthusiasm for design to potential clients. With strong support over the years from major owner/builders, she has carved out her own area of design service.

Part Five

PROMOTING YOUR PRACTICE

D

ESIGN is a relatively new profession. Yet its value is being recognized by the rest of the commercial world at a remarkable rate. Designers and architects have captured the public imagination in ways that computer programmers never will.

All that makes it easier and more pleasant for you to promote your practice than it has ever been. Yet it is no secret that as individuals, we are often quite reticent about "blowing our own horn." In groups we are getting better: ASID, IBD, AIGA, AIA, IDSA, APA, and ASLA, to name some of the largest design organizations. Such groups have learned to use design award programs, public relations, and political action to every member's advantage.

The point of this section of the book is to help you get over the shyness that may have kept you from sharing your firm's gifts with a wider audience than the one that came in "over the transom." This section is also aimed at helping you find inexpensive ways to develop promotional materials. Thick, glossy brochures often don't accomplish enough to justify their cost. They sometimes even work to a design firm's disadvantage: A nonprofit or public institution client may wonder who ultimately pays the cost of the elaborate four-color "packages" blithely handed to each member of its board during a presentation. Remember that in the end promotional materials can never replace the value of a warm and sincere personal contact for successful marketing.

Chapter Fifteen
CHOOSING VISUAL MATERIALS

To many designers, the presentation materials are the most important element in selling the job; at least it is the part they like best. That's understandable: The pictures are visual testimony to one's skill and esthetic commitment; there is always a quiet surge of pride after seeing the slides of one's work flashed onto a screen or neatly arranged in a portfolio. Unfortunately, that self-satisfaction has very little to do with winning commissions these days. Your presentation of completed work must be seen objectively, as a tool developed to influence others. Ask someone whose judgment you trust whether your current slide show, for instance, presents your firm as a responsive, resourceful service organization or as one more interested in esthetic recognition. If your friend has any doubts, be assured that potential clients are likely to have a much stronger negative response. That is why the emphasis here is on keeping your client's needs in mind when assembling your presentation.

COMPARING PRESENTATION MEDIA

Slides versus presentation boards: From a marketing or selling point of view, most of the designers participating in this book see slides, if used at all, as suitable only for large meetings. Gordon Perry makes the distinction: "When I was working with smaller companies and interviewing on a one-to-one basis, a flat book full of 8 × 10 photographs was quite successful; now that I present to larger groups—usually in conference rooms—I find that slides can be impressive, especially when combined with printed material that I can leave with the potential clients."

Jeanne Hartnett's firm, which mainly serves corporate and institutional clients, uses slides as its main form of selling. They often mix staff-taken shots of interior design work in progress with finished slides by a professional photographer for extra impact. The show is specifically set up to reflect the particular client's interests and offered in as personal a way as possible in order to build rapport with them.

Unless that effort is consistently made, however, slide shows can cause more problems than opportunities. Bill Koster points out: "Slides are a damned nuisance to prepare, to set up at the interview, and then ask the clients to rearrange themselves in order to view—especially in a limited-time slot. Turning the lights off is a sure way to lose touch with the audience." Ken Arutunian has "moved away from slide presenta-

Compact slide projectors with integral screens enable you to show slides of your work in a prospect's office with no need to set up or adjust the lighting.

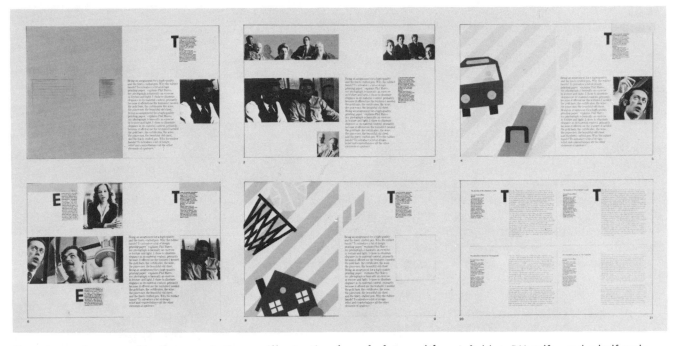

Infield + D'Astolfo used a half-scale dummy of a proposed annual report to help their clients understand how this twelve-page sequence would look when printed.

tions toward personalized presentations—illustration board plates with plans, photos, perspectives, and captions—that deal with the project in question rather than with our firm and its experience. These boards are prepared in the office and help us keep costs down—the expense is more in employee time than in costly photographic materials."

Judith Chafee says: "We arrange our work in 11 × 14 portfolios, one or two per project. These acetate sleeves, bound with white spine, include publication of the project, presentation drawings sufficient to orient the viewer, and original photography. This format gives us the flexibility, of editing the presentation to the most appropriate material, even of editing during the course of a meeting, as the potential client's priorities become clearer."

Gail Biddison notes: "Much to our surprise 18 × 24 inch presentation boards of completed interiors jobs or ones in progress are our most successful tools in winning jobs. There is something immediate and tactile about these boards that has proven to be appealing to potential clients. Use of a consistent format for preparing the boards gives a sense of comparing apples to apples; it points up differences in one solution over another better than slides can."

Obviously each designer must decide which medium works best for his or her needs, and like Gordon Perry, you may decide to have both available, depending on where and to whom you are presenting. The simpler and more concise a slide show, the better it is; slides showing plans and other details must be drawn especially for that purpose—bold and simple. Images that look fine on paper are often too delicate to read clearly when magnified and lit from behind in a projector. Presentation boards also require careful planning to convey their message to a conference room audience.

DOING INEXPENSIVE VISUAL MATERIALS

FOR THE ABOVE REASONS, this section will concentrate on presentation boards rather than slide shows. One advantage that you have over other businesses that must describe their services is that you can hire students part-time or during the summer to fabricate your displays or keep them up to date. Skills they are developing in school come in very handy for your marketing purposes. That does not mean that preparation of your boards should be a low-priority or ad hoc process. It merely means that once an overall format has been decided upon, the preparation work can be done by your staff, with little of your time required.

Naturally, the graphic system or grid that you specify is the most demanding part of the job. You may even want to have a graphic design consultant review your sketches before settling on a system. Study magazine formats that appeal to you. While they are serving a different purpose, layouts that seem appropriate to displaying your work can be easily adapted.

Consider arranging your boards to tell a story about how your solutions to design problems come from solving a client's needs. Be sure to provide adequate labels, but remember that almost no one likes to read a lot of explanatory copy. The pictures should be big and clearly supportive of the points you are making. Even comic books may hold lessons for you in punching home ideas with humor and easy comprehension. Strong visual style seems so widely accepted these days that you have an enormous latitude in which to work: from white illustration board with images neatly organized and labeled to richly colored and embellished surfaces that capture the complexity of the most sophisticated postmodern design philosophy. If you keep in mind that you are selling professional services that solve people's design problems, then the appropriate amount of "fun" versus old-fashioned consistency will no doubt be apparent as you design the boards.

MARKETING THROUGH GRAPHICS

EVERYTHING YOU SEND out of the office will also be judged by a potential client on its appearance. We all know that, but far too often we never quite get around to doing anything about it. If you designed your letterhead in 1970 and it looked great then, chances are it doesn't these days. Whether you are deciding to undertake a comprehensive marketing program as outlined in earlier chapters or just considering a slightly stepped-up effort, think about revamping your office graphics program at the same time.

Advertising has had as profound an effect on design as design has upon advertising. Twenty years ago, architects were committed to standardized graphics for job signs, letterheads, and building signage—Helvetica seemed to answer all our needs. Partly because there was a lot more construction activity in those days, architects and designers in related fields found that it paid to present a unified image. Today, visual differentiation—which is of course what advertising is about—is needed to win attention and jobs for designers in a much slower economy. Therefore, while it is true that most designers can produce adequate if predictable graphic solutions all by themselves, we may have reached a point when the one professional service we can't afford to ignore is graphic design itself. Architect Alfredo De Vido agrees. He uses Whitehouse and Katz as his graphics consultant. "Architects do crappy graphics," he says, "I can spot homemade letterheads a mile away."

Identity and image are the two issues that graphics professionals are trained to address. The graphic designer develops the image that captures the business identity of the client. It is an organization's intent and spirit—its identity—that must be captured; it is a rare firm in our field that can analyze itself without help. Yet for its marketing program to express the essence of a design firm, the visual components—its image—must be precisely crafted. The goal, says Warren Infield,

A graphic designer (in this case Pamela Waters) approaches each logo by considering the uses to which it will be put and the effect sought by the client. The chess pieces (below) were created for the giant board above a Manhattan office plaza (page 130).

"should be a graphic presentation that is derived from and suited to the client firm's own design work. It conveys a memorable quality without overwhelming the substance of the communication."

Typography, for instance, is an exceedingly subtle element in graphics. Most of us are only now willing to consider a serif typeface for use in one of our designs. Graphic designers are familiar with forty or fifty different serif alphabets, using them as needed to isolate nuances of feeling otherwise lost in the composition. Helvetica had become a graphic formula that was usually applied whether appropriate or not—a remarkable exception to the designer's ideal of deriving every part of the solution from an overall concept with no preconceptions.

There are other, more practical reasons to work with graphic designers. The printing business is as complicated as building construction and a great deal more precise. Graphics professionals bring a broad sense of the available techniques to each job they do, matching design needs to printing options that are economically and functionally appropriate. They know, for instance, which printers can do two-color work almost as inexpensively as a single-color job. They know that three colors are sometimes more expensive than four. Graphics designers keep tabs on the cost of dozens of different kinds and weights of paper. Even so, they almost always get several bids on a job since printers will sometimes do work virtually at cost to keep the presses rolling. And it is all done with attention to detail on a scale that designers in the building field can never hope to achieve.

BUYING PROFESSIONAL PHOTOGRAPHY

Aᴌᴍᴏsᴛ ᴇᴠᴇʀʏ ᴅᴇsɪɢɴᴇʀ has learned to recognize the value of professional photography. After all, with the exception of certain graphic design projects, we sell with pictures rather than with the actual objects we design. Since many of us also enjoy using a camera to record our work as it is being realized, we have no trouble distinguishing between informal and more serious photographs.

Yet for all of that, you may not have experience in actually engaging one of these experts to do photographs for marketing purposes. In many parts of the United States there are no professionals nearby who specialize in architectural (which includes interiors) or product photography. Your decision to commission work, therefore, may mean dealing with an individual by telephone and paying travel expenses in addition to day rates that, at $600 to $1,200, will no doubt give you pause. Fortunately, by carefully noting the credit lines attached to photographs you admire in the various journals, you can easily come up with your own shortlist of candidates. Since the photographers themselves are always on the move, you may find whomever you call quite willing to discuss a visit either directly to your door or as part of a trip through your region planned in the future.

Thinking through your needs before contacting photographers will help make negotiations more productive. Perhaps, if you need several days' shooting in a fairly small geographic area, the day rate can be lowered significantly. If you can describe fairly precisely what shots you need, that will cut costs, since certain equipment may not be required.

An added reason for contacting photographers with a national reputation has to do with publication of your work. Sometimes the photographer will be willing to work for a fraction of his or her normal rate because the pictures can also be sold to a magazine with which the individual works. But don't count on that. Even with a dozen articles

Even lighting, parallel verticals, clear rendering of materials, and expression of depth in the shot by Stan Ries of an interior by Voorsanger and Mills illustrates the value of professional photography.

Photo: Stan Ries/ESTO

appearing this past year on their work, Voorsanger and Mills say that they spent 2½ percent of their gross annual income on photography.

For other marketing purposes—slide shows or work-in-progress and record photographs—you may decide to find a local photographer or a student who has an interest in gaining experience in shooting interiors or furniture or other designed products in a studio. You may even want to do the work yourself. The cost will be considerably lower and you may be quite satisfied with the results. The important thing is that excellent photographs are extremely valuable as marketing tools and, if properly used, will generate far more money than they cost you.

EXPLORING VIDEO AS A SELLING TOOL

THE MARKETING POTENTIAL of video has yet to be tapped by designers. Now that many businesses use video cassette recorders (VCR) as part of their sales programs, it is practical to send them a cassette of your own, knowing that there is a very good chance it will be viewed out of curiosity, if nothing else.

Video is primarily a "people medium." You will be wise to use it for interviews, showing that your former clients and their employees or customers are very happy with the facilities or product that you have designed for them. Don't bother shooting the finished project directly. Video is most effective "animating," that is, panning; good quality 8 × 10 photographs show the completed job.

A twenty-minute, half-inch videotape program can be put together for under $2,000, especially if the camera work, narrating, and editing are done by a member of your firm. The equipment can be rented from most dealers if you do not wish to invest in it. You can also get information and technical assistance from dealers.

For even broader use, a script that discusses your project in a somewhat larger context and includes a bit of supporting documentary material—such as "Humane Housing for the Elderly" or "Industrial Design Tackles Safety Problems in the Home"—could find a place on cable television, at conferences, and in schools. By soft-pedaling your involvement in the design but including a prominent credit at the end, you can build that image of expertise so important to marketing in a specialized design field. Unlike slide shows or presentation boards, video is still such a novelty that less-than-professional craftsmanship is acceptable if the content enlightens or amuses its audience.

Issues to Negotiate with a Photographer

1. Method of charging for services, including travel expenses.

2. Method of charging for prints and slides.

3. Experience with jobs like yours.

4. References in your city or region.

5. Availability and scheduling.

6. Equipment and lighting options.

7. Rights and ownership of photographs.

8. Publication possibilities.

Chapter Sixteen
CREATING PRINTED MATERIALS

FOR SOME REASON, designers often decide to put a lot of money into printed promotional materials and hope the rest of marketing will take care of itself. As early parts of this book make clear, marketing not only doesn't happen without effort but costs a good deal as well. Thus, there is good reason to budget most of your marketing funds for lead-finding, contacts' travel and entertainment, and looking for ways to stretch the dollars left for brochures, portfolios, and other handouts. A common rule is to allocate $1 for such handouts for every $2 or $3 you spend lead-finding and selling.

For designers it can be a stimulating task to devise inexpensive materials for self-use. Not only are you sensitive to the visual possibilities inherent in modest graphic techniques, but you have work to present that can speak for itself without verbal embellishment.

SELECTING THE APPROPRIATE FORMAT

THE BOUND, elegantly printed brochures that large design firms use to dazzle corporate boards of directors are a poor choice for any firm that has limited funds for marketing. The idea, if you are seeking commissions from clients who themselves prepare elaborate annual reports and business documents, is to convey the same elegance with much simpler means. Jean Hartnett's firm found itself in that position and solved the problem with a sixty-page spiral-bound brochure assembled in its office from components as needed. The printed components cost about $5,000 in 1982 for a thousand sets.

The cost-effective alternative to brochures is the portfolio—a handsomely produced cover or "kit" that encloses a packet of staff and project description sheets, reprints, and client lists. Because these components can be readily assembled just before mailing or presentation, flexibility, selectivity, modularity, and ease of updating are all advantages of such a system. Choice of heavy-weight, coated or embossed paper stock for the kit is generally within the means of a small firm. Avoid complex die-cutting and assembly for the pockets in which accompanying sheets are placed.

De Vido has simplified it by having a pocket of the same paper stock made and glued onto his cover by someone in the office. Radford-Biddison and UDA, among others, have had folders describing professional qualifications printed that match the kit itself. These are one-piece, single-fold sheets in one or two colors on heavy, glossy paper that include photographs of the principals, describe their background, and set out a brief statement of the firm's approach to design. In some cases photographs of complete jobs or line drawings of process sketches are also shown. Along with the kit itself, these folders cost about $3,000 for a thousand copies.

Others—Pamela Waters and Jordan/Mitchell, for instance—avoid the kit altogether. They just put material in a standard manila envelope.

PREPARING INEXPENSIVE PRINT PIECES

THERE IS NO mystery about how to save money on printing work: Keep it simple. Warren Infield explains that the fewer distinct operations required to produce the finished result, the lower the cost. "Printers or their reps are always available to help you simplify design ideas or work out alternatives." Sometimes they have equipment that cuts labor so effectively that you can afford special effects you would not have thought possible on a small budget. For instance, use crisp executive typewriter script instead of photo-offset typefaces to avoid the cost of that operation (a substantial savings). Cuts (printing image) of line drawings are less expensive than halftones made from photographs; perspective renderings that consist of dot and line patterns reproduce very well using this method. Mezzotint is the technique for reducing photographs to line cuts, a less expensive process than making a halftone.

Naturally, if you do use photographs, avoid four-color printing because so many expensive production operations are required. Simple geometric layouts are the best bet so long as they are flexible enough to minimize the "loving hands at home" effect in amateur pasteups. In the end you get what you pay for; the best advice may be to work out a graphic system (such as a layout grid and type families for body text and heads) with a professional consultant that can be upgraded as you can afford it. That way there will be a sense of consistency among your promotional materials.

Frank D'Astolfo's sketch illustrates eight basic formats for brochures, ranging from a single sheet of paper folded one or more times to bound examples. The lower row contains (left to right) a die-cut folder with integral pocket, a "perfect-bound" or stapled booklet, a three-ring binder (wire and plastic spiral bindings fall into this category), and a hardcover-in-a-box version (naturally the most expensive).

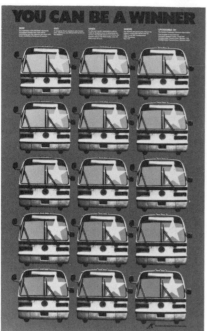

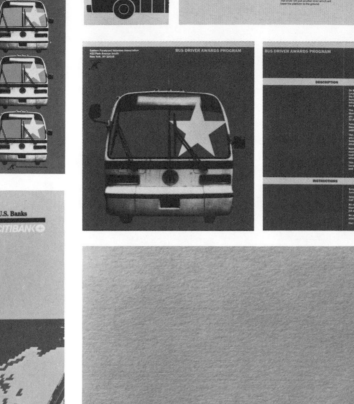

MONOCID

Examples by Infield + D'Astolfo of brochure and other graphic options are shown clockwise from upper left: poster on enameled stock, double-fold and triple-fold two-color mailers sized for a No. 10 envelope, an embossed folder of charcoal paper with color photograph cards inserted in the pocket, two spreads of logos from Infield + D'Astolfo's own spiral-bound brochure, and a cover from a three-color stapled booklet.

DESCRIBING YOUR
PROJECTS EFFECTIVELY

THE MOST IMPORTANT component of your portfolio is the individual project description sheet. For the prospective client these sheets are the most important element in the packet you send. They reveal more about your firm's personality than any philosophical statement you can write.

Stress the project's visual elements rather than a long written description. Shelter magazines like *House & Garden* provide a good model for the layout of project description pages. Notice that the words are usually divided between "decks," a ten-to-fifteen word headline that tells why the design solution is worth studying, and captions, the "twenty-five words or less" used to point out specific features of each photograph or drawing. Captions should spell out clearly what the client's design problem was and how you helped solve it.

The examples shown here, from De Vido's portfolio, make consistent use of these magazine layout concepts. Each sheet also has a table in the upper right-hand corner that gives the client's name, location, completion date, size, and cost of the house. De Vido combines clearly drawn plans, professional photographs, and, when useful, simplified technical drawings, to offer a series of comparative studies from which potential clients can learn a great deal about how his firm operates.

MAKING WORDS
WORK FOR YOU

EVEN BEFORE we knew about right-brain and left-brain skills, it was clear that designers usually have trouble writing clearly and concisely about their own work. The problem is not just the mechanics of writing—grammar, syntax, spelling, and vocabulary—but it also has to do with the subjective association we have with our designs. Few designers, even after they learn how important writing is to the business side of the profession, are willing to go back and master the basics of language that they ignored in elementary school. However, the lack of objectivity is no doubt a much more serious problem when it comes to writing for marketing purposes.

That is why, as part of the commitment to marketing you may be planning to make, you should consider finding a consultant who can write letters and project description copy as well as you can design. Some of you are lucky enough to have a secretary who can not only spell but write a sensible business letter. That person may well be so involved in your firm's economics already that he or she would make an excellent marketing-support person. If that is not the case, keep an eye on the bylines in your local newspaper. When you spot a writing style that you enjoy reading, call up the reporter and ask if he or she would be interested in a part-time role as your editor and advisor on using words for marketing. Once you have worked out the basic format for your marketing program, you probably will need no more than two or three hours a month consultation. Thus, at $20 to $25 per hour, you can have a valuable resource for both language skills and clear thinking without a big investment.

Making words work for you means choosing them as carefully and as economically as you choose the colors for your designs. A trained writer recognizes the importance of brevity in communicating, and knows how to get ideas across directly but without sacrificing the appropriate style. Business people will just *not* read a letter or printed material that rambles or fails to make its point clearly. Since successful marketing

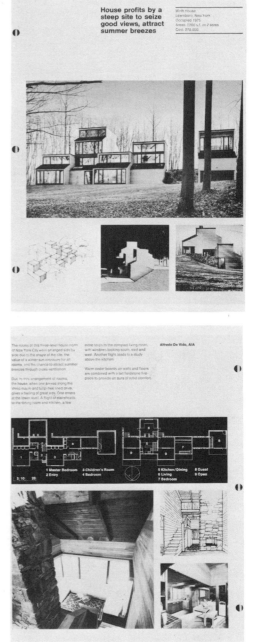

Front and back of a project description sheet are from De Vido's brochure. Professional-quality photographs, easily readable drawings, and well-organized text make these pages impressive to potential clients.

communication requires that the reader not only absorb the message but have a positive emotional response to it, the need for clarity and grace in the language of your mailings is apparent.

The way that words are used in shelter magazines can be helpful in understanding the value of clear, concise writing. If you count the words in a typical article that accompanies photographs and drawings of a well-designed project, you will see that the writer has only 500 or 1,000 with which to describe the background of the project, the process followed in its design, the materials and fabrication, and so on. Each sentence is short and uses the simplest possible grammar. There is very little jargon and what does appear will be explained so that everyone understands. There is a generous tone and the project is almost always described in positive terms. The effect is that you look at the pictures again with greater awareness, knowledge, and appreciation. And at the same time, if the writing is well done, you forget about the words *completely*. That should be your goal in writing for marketing: to create a powerful effect with words that are essentially invisible.

SPREADING THE NEWS

AS A MARKETING TOOL, newsletters can be a useful way of keeping clients and prospects abreast of what you are doing. Screen every item to see if it meets the test of evidence of high performance by your firm in terms of design quality and successful cost and schedule control as well as added evidence that you are a responsible, progressive firm with satisfied clients. Don't send a newsletter out more than three to four times a year, and avoid using it as a vehicle for staff gossip that best belongs in a house organ.

The newsletter is not something to undertake without thorough planning, especially as to how it relates to the rest of your promoting and selling. In fact, you will be wise to wait until your marketing plan has evolved over a year or more so that you will understand clearly to whom you are addressing the newsletter, how frequently it should be published, and how elaborately it should be designed and produced. As the replacement for your present periodic mailings, it can be immensely more effective than a sporadic dispatch of news releases, tearsheets, and Christmas cards. A consistent pattern of mailing dates is what distinguishes newsletters from other forms of periodic communication.

Your newsletter can be as simple as a single typewritten sheet that is photocopied, folded, and stapled—a self-mailer. There is a substantial range in production cost between that and the newspaperlike printed folder sent out every six months by Jaffe Acoustics (shown here). Furthermore, the cost of preparing such a document includes, besides printing, the efforts of a graphic designer and an experienced writer.

It takes more than writing skill to present your own work as news. It calls for objectivity and journalistic instinct. What seems like hot news to you may or may not interest the thousand other people to whom your newsletter will be sent. The question is how to present your news so that those who get the mailing will read it carefully, remember your name, and if you are lucky, mention it to someone else.

Ann Boyar, marketing director for Jaffe Acoustics, has worked on newsletters in other fields. She develops the layout and general copy ideas with a free-lance promotional advertising consultant. Then she hones the copy with Christopher Jaffe to make it as informative as possible for the readership. The first three issues each focus on a general acoustical topic with an essay by Jaffe, a reprinted newspaper article that mentions the firm prominently, a table that clarifies specific acous-

The Jaffe Acoustics Report is a newsletter that offers the reader news, technical information, and relevant visual examples in an inexpensive yet professional-looking fashion.

tical data, a list of concert halls or other recently completed projects, two or three photographs, and a couple of line drawings. Printed on beige text offset paper with sepia ink, each issue of four 8½ × 11 pages costs Jaffe $3,500 for about 2,500 copies. Between 1,500 and 1,800 go to names on their mailing list, and the rest are used for general promotion.

Another format, much more simple, is used by UDA for periodic mailings and general promotion. They use a high-quality photocopier to prepare a three- or four-page package on their letterhead describing a recent project: a 300-word description followed by pen-and-ink sketches and appropriate plans. Since they send this material to people with whom they have worked before or who know them well, no further explanation is needed.

ADVERTISING YOUR SERVICES

As THE RESULT of U.S. Justice Department initiatives over the past decade, all constraints against advertising by architects have been removed. The other design disciplines never had any. Still, design professionals have been extremely reticent about using paid advertising to promote their services.

Three of the sixteen firms participating in this book do advertise. However, these designers have limited themselves to professional services-type advertisements. Ralph Appelbaum and Gordon Perry place small ads in convention and trade show programs in the museum management and product manufacturing fields, respectively. Appelbaum usually chooses an isometric rendering of a recent exhibition installation and a brief list of current clients. He reports that other exhibition designers often use pictures of themselves and their staffs in such ads.

Advertisements can be informative yet dignified and visually attractive as this example from a museum journal makes clear.

His experience has shown that publicity is more effective in generating prospects than this type of advertising.

Jaffe Associates has had such positive results from its marketing program that they have chosen to reduce their advertising budget. The 1982 marketing budget set aside $10,000 for advertising, most of which went for full-page space in *Symphony* magazine. The format was a large photograph of a recently completed concert hall interior already familiar to the magazine's readers with the single statement, "Jaffe Acoustics, acousticians of record." In 1983, the firm is cutting back to one-quarter page advertisements and putting the savings into more specific promotion.

These days, the issue for designers is not whether to advertise or not. The matter for your consideration is how to develop an advertising program that grows out of your marketing plan and that in turn is reinforced by it. When and where to advertise involves questions that call for expert advice. If you are contemplating anything more complex than a small, traditional professional advertisement, therefore, seek experienced counsel before making any commitments. For a thorough discussion of advertising that applies to all design disciplines, see "Advertising the Architect's Services: Moving from Legal and Ethical Controversy to Marketing Strategy," by Stephen A. Kliment in the January 1978 *Architectural Record.*

Nathaniel Curtis advertises his broad record in institutional architecture to design professionals he hopes will retain him because of his experience in marketing.

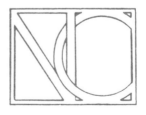

Chapter Seventeen
USING PROMOTION MATERIALS TO WIN JOBS

SEEING YOUR SHELVES full of your promotional materials may bolster your ego. However, distributing them according to plan is just as vital as doing them in the first place.

BLOWING YOUR OWN HORN IS O.K.

ONE REASON for beginning the marketing program with a self-analysis of your firm is to appreciate—in as objective a way as possible—the skill and talent gathered in your organization. Very few of us combine, as Frank Lloyd Wright did, great talent as a designer and as a business promoter. Many who have creative gifts and propose bold visual schemes are exceptionally timid about exercising initiative in the marketplace. An inhibition against self-advertisement affects many of us so that however hungry our ego may be for recognition, the super-ego says, "No, we must be dignified as professionals—even a bit aloof." Not every designer has that problem, of course, but for those who do, the idea of pushing oneself forward to win jobs is very painful.

That is why, when you begin to market your services, it is important to keep in mind the reason for seeking publicity and public attention. If you understand fully that the point is less for personal gratification than for impersonal business development, then your shyness will be put into proper perspective. Gere Kavanaugh has the right idea: "If as a designer you feel strongly about what your office is doing, you should speak at as many gatherings as possible. It's valuable because your name precedes you on program announcements and advertisements for the occasion. That gives you a lot of credibility."

"It has taken me a while to be comfortable about putting myself forward," says Will Ching, "but now I do not shy away from talking about my firm."

GETTING PUBLICITY

"PUBLICITY" IS the process of putting your firm's name before, first of all, potential clients and, secondly, those who might influence potential clients. There are many events (see chart on page 147) that can be turned into publicity for marketing purposes if you are alert to their potential. Many of the larger design offices use public relations counselors on a consulting basis and you may wish to investigate sources of professional assistance yourself. The contacts with the various branches of the media that these people cultivate are invaluable, especially if you are interested in reaching broad, general audiences. Your own contacts with the professional design media, however, may well be better than theirs.

The actual mechanics of public relations work are not so complicated that a well-structured design firm needs a great deal of help to carry them out. The press or news release is the primary tool and a distribution plan is the means for making it work. Whether you ask a PR person to help you get started or consult journalism reference books, you will discover that a press release should contain the elements in the accompanying box.

Press releases are not easy to write, to be sure, but the technique can be mastered readily with a bit of patience.

Don't send out a press release unless you have something worthwhile to say. "Worthwhile" means a major commission, a major design award, a major promotion. Avoid peppering the news media with a flood of insignificant news. You will soon wear out your welcome.

Few design firms will send out more than a dozen press releases a year, but even at that rate a distribution plan is valuable. Some organizations use news releases as a form of periodic communication with former and prospective clients; you may wish to use them that way in addition to sending them to members of the press—a multipurpose and relatively inexpensive way to keep people you care about informed. Thus there may be two major categories in your distribution plan and, within those, subheadings that enable you to select which kinds of clients and which branches of the press to whom you mail the release. The general list described under mailing programs (see page 102) can be easily adapted for this purpose. On big projects, you will want to coordinate publicity efforts with your client, the contractors, and relevant suppliers. It is crucial for success that the editors to whom you send releases receive a follow-up call within a few days of the mailing.

Judith Chafee has made excellent use of Tucson newspapers and regional magazines to place her work and the ideas behind it before the public. UDA did a large planning project in Warren, Ohio, to which the *Tribune Chronicle* devoted a twenty-page supplement—including a questionnaire for reader response. The Pittsburgh firm has also mounted a nine-project exhibition of its work that appeared in Cincinnati and Columbus, Ohio, university art galleries.

City magazines are, as mentioned earlier, generally receptive to suggestions for feature articles with a design theme. (See the next section for design magazines.) The trade or business magazines that potential clients read as part of their business also deserve mention again in this context. Well-written contributed (nonpaid) articles that illuminate relevant design issues are often irresistible to thrifty editors of such magazines—for example, an article on the use of color in hospitals in a journal read by hospital administrators.

Radio and television talk shows, TV news features (the renovated interior of an old downtown building, for instance), and various forms of cable television programming are all worth exploring. Identify the shows you would like to appear on, and then write to the program manager in care of the station and suggest a topic you feel the station's audience would find attractive and why you are the right person to take part. Remember many local stations, and nearly all cable programs, are desperately short of good programming.

Whatever the medium, the important test for publicity efforts is: Will prospects or those who influence prospects be reached? One last, very important item: As Pamela Waters points out, always be sure your client gets a credit and, if possible, a plug for contributing to "good design."

News Release Tips

1. **Telephone contact:** After the words "For Immediate Release," the name and business telephone of someone who can offer callers further information.

2. **Headline:** A five- to eight-word statement that tells the story in a clear and appealing way.

3. **Lead (opening paragraph):** One or two readable sentences (up to 50 words) that include the 5 Ws and an H (what, when, who, why, where, and how) as well as the name of your firm—in short the main information stated in newsworthy fashion.

4. **Body of the release:** Further information about the event including a natural-sounding quote by an appropriate spokesperson for your firm. The release should be no more than two double-spaced typed pages total.

Publicity Events and Appropriate Media

1. Business developments (new partners, joint ventures, retirements, financial news): Business sections of newspapers and city magazines in your marketing area, radio and television business news programs.

2. Office relocation or expansion: Real estate sections of newspapers or magazines in the specific community and in your marketing area.

3. Key staff additions and promotions: Real estate and/or business sections of newspapers in your marketing area as well as the hometowns of individuals involved, regional and national design magazines.

4. Major new jobs: Real estate and/or business sections as above as well as local, regional, and national publications in the fields relevant to your commission.

5. Completed projects: Business and features editors of newspapers and magazines in your marketing area and (if visually exceptional) television news staffs, regional, and national design magazines.

6. Lectures, school talks, and panel discussions: News and feature sections of newspapers and magazines in your marketing area (including announcements beforehand with a request for coverage).

7. Appearances on cable television or radio talk shows: Radio/television section of affected newspapers asking for special notice in their calendars.

8. Publication of articles or projects in the national architectural, interior design, graphics, or other professional press: News section of affected newspapers, including a black-and-white photograph, if relevant.

9. Invitations to participate in competitions and prizes won: News and cultural (arts) sections of appropriate newspapers, magazines, and radio/television stations.

10. Foreign or cross-continental business travel: Business and social notes section of appropriate newspapers (don't ignore this sort of item—it can look quite impressive in print).

11. Foreign or otherwise distinguished visitors to your firm: Business and social notes sections of appropriate newspapers.

12. Social activities, especially benefits and fund-raisers: Social notes section of appropriate newspapers.

100 students attend fifth annual career day at New Jersey design firm's offices

Princeton, N.J.—A group of 100 area students and their parents turned out for the fifth annual career day sponsored by local design firm, The Hillier Group.

Students were shown slide presentations on the history of architecture, toured the facility, and met individually with working architects and interior designers. Representatives from New York Institute of Technology, New Jersey Institute of Technology, Pratt Institute, the University of Arkansas, Mercer County Community College, Howard University, Kent State, and Temple University were also on-hand.

Developed to increase students' exposure to working design professionals, career day has proved to be a valuable resource for aspiring space planners.

Says Hillier Group president J. Robert Hillier, "Since we began offering career day, many schools have instituted in-depth career counselling programs for their design students."

Credit: Courtesy Contract Magazine

An imaginatively structured event can bring publicity benefits when reported to relevant professional magazines with a well-written news release.

GETTING MORE
OUT OF PUBLICATION

EVEN THOUGH it doesn't reach your client prospects directly, publication in the national design (and in some cases shelter and general interest) magazines can be productive from the marketing point of view. Edward Mills, whose firm of Voorsanger and Mills is featured in perhaps a dozen articles a year, finds that other architects and interior designers, who for some reason must refuse a commission, will sometimes recommend him just because they admire what they've seen of the office's work in magazines. Alfredo De Vido, another widely published architect, has gotten similar referrals from design professionals who do not design houses. So there are times when publication in the "mags" has a direct marketing benefit.

By itself, however, publication in the professional press is far less effective than you may think. Only in rare cases do potential clients read design magazines regularly or when seeking to commission a project. Architects featured, for instance, in "Record Houses" seldom get calls from interested parties. Articles in *Architectural Digest*, a consumer-oriented magazine, on the other hand, sometimes bring calls and mail in alarming quantities. The same holds true in the graphic interior and industrial design publications. *Corporate Design* and *Facilities Design & Management* magazines were founded, as a matter of fact, to bridge that gap. They are aimed at an audience of facilities managers and other corporate executives.

Nonetheless, designers will persist in seeking publication in periodicals read by their peers. Therefore, a few words on how to succeed are in order. Let's assume you feel quite strongly that a recent piece of your work is "publishable." The procedure is to assemble a "package" of material and information to send to editors of appropriate magazines (if you decide to send them to more than one at a time, be prepared to call off all the others at once as soon as one gives you a *firm* commitment of publication).

Photographs are the overwhelmingly important element—editors publish pictures of design projects, not the works themselves. Many magazines will say that candid or polaroid shots will do. That is questionable on two counts. First if the forms and colors of your design are misrepresented or undervalued by weak photos, the project may be rejected. Second if the editor receives a set of stunning professional photographs, he or she is very likely to find a use for them because they are in hand and free to the magazine. Six photographs (with one or two slides perhaps showing overall views) are usually enough to sell the design quality, so don't spend a lot on detail and nearly duplicate photos. Crisply drawn ink plans/sections/details that explain how the design works should also be included (don't send a big packet of technical drawings unless asked). Finally, a one- or two-page typed statement explaining the design goals, process, and execution stages is necessary along with all relevant credits and product information. (The latter can be very important if one of your suppliers happens to be a big advertiser in the magazine.)

Now, let's assume your work is going to be published. The part that matters *most* is arranging for copies ahead of time. You are taking a chance to do it before you see the article, it's true, but most design magazines do their best to present projects in a good light. Even if the layout and/or production looks terrible when you finally see it, prospective clients will still be impressed because the publication is seen as an objective third party that endorses your work. Mills, who certainly knows from experience, says, "For presentations we mostly depend on magazine tearsheets showing our projects as they appeared in print. They are the best promotional materials and cost about 50 cents each."

Incidentally, the magazine may offer you twenty-five to fifty sets of "tearsheets"—unbound pages from the magazine—free. Those will be gone in a couple of weeks, and therefore a sustained marketing program justifies an additional investment in reprints. In short, it is the acquisition of those beautifully printed, glossy-paper copies of the article for distribution to future prospects that makes all your efforts toward publication worthwhile.

CAPITALIZING ON DESIGN AWARD PROGRAMS

ONE OF THE MOST clever marketing ideas that the design professions have come up with so far are "design award programs." Organizations of designers—local and national—offer annual opportunities for their members to submit work for judgment by well-known peers who then award prizes generously. Nowhere has this concept flourished as in the graphic design field.

"We regularly submit work to prestigious, juried shows," says Warren Infield, "and have had our work published in national and international publications such as the AIGA, Graphis, and New York Art Directors annuals. Overall this is a cost-effective way to stay in the public eye (entry fees are small except for some school and hospital design programs), to gain peer recognition, and to help the firm name become familiar. Awards imply success; clients understand the value of this success and a certain credibility results." The prizes have another unexpected virtue, Infield and D'Astolfo have discovered. The corporate officers who commission prize-winning designers benefit as well, within their own hierarchy, when the projects they have worked on are recognized by outside opinion. Another benefit of winning an award is the free publicity arranged for by the sponsoring group or association.

In the architecture and interior design fields, the Progressive Architecture, Record Houses, Record Interiors, as well as Interiors award programs have all made valuable contributions to the development of designer careers. The marketing value of these awards has been less clearly perceived by architects and interior designers than by graphic designers, but that is changing according to Ray Gindroz of UDA: "I have been interested in the reaction from clients and potential clients to our 1983 Progressive Architecture Design Award. There has been good press coverage in Pittsburgh and many people have called us. Our clients in Richmond, Virginia, have had even better press coverage and have found it to be enormously useful in supporting their urban redevelopment program. That's why we continue to feel that awards programs are a useful part of marketing."

If you can keep ego satisfaction separate from these pragmatic considerations, entering awards programs will be a lot easier for you, in emotional terms, and probably more productive in the long run.

SHAKING HANDS AT CONVENTIONS AND TRADE SHOWS

IT'S A RARE DESIGNER who loves to "glad-hand" people the way politicians do. Most have trouble going to conferences and aggressively greeting strangers. Yet there is no doubt of its value in securing new commissions. The decision-makers of the field are gathered in one place for a few days, they are open to new ideas, and they are in a mood to talk.

Ralph Appelbaum, one of those "nonmarketers," still manages to create a strong presence at national and international conferences on museum management and planning. By advertising in the booklet handed to each delegate and appearing on panels dealing with exhibition design, he moves discreetly among the leaders in the field, strengthening earlier acquaintances and using them to broaden his network. Because he has committed his firm to raising the standards of scientific exhibition design, he is able to get past his shyness to work for the good of his firm and the discipline as a whole.

William Koster gets the last word. He too has learned to put shyness aside in favor of assertive marketing promotion: "Municipal architecture is a field where there is always the possibility of multiple projects for the same client: fire stations, recreation centers, senior citizen centers, city halls, and so on. Also each of these building types has its own inter-city network—fire chiefs talk to fire chiefs at their conventions, mayors talk to mayors at theirs. When I show up there, I always find a former client who is happy to take me around to meet his peers."

In marketing being in the right place at the right time makes the difference.

Things to Do	*Things to Avoid*
Learn to tell everyone you meet how good your firm's work is.	**Printed brochures** that can't be modified as your firm grows and develops.
Keep your audience—not yourself—in mind when preparing promotion materials.	**Written statements** that cannot be easily grasped by the people to whom you are sending them.
Choose your presentation medium with an eye toward the space in which you'll be talking—slides for big rooms, boards for smaller ones.	**Promotion material** that is overly elaborate, especially if it substantially exceeds the prospects' expectations.
Order additional copies of articles about your work *before* the magazine is published.	**On the other hand,** amateurish or old-fashioned looking folders and other descriptive pieces.
Work with consultants—graphic designers, writers, photographers, public relations counselors—to help you do a better job of presenting your practice.	**Presentations** that do not allow for maximum interaction by the prospective client.
Prepare press releases about your firm's accomplishments and follow up by calling the editors to whom you send them.	**Advertising** that is not integrated into your marketing program.
Organize and send an appropriate form of periodic communication to former clients and other friends of your firm.	**False modesty** about your work and half-hearted efforts at promotion.
Encourage former clients to help promote your office.	**Not sending** your promotion material out every chance you get.

Appendices

A. MARKETING WITH MICROCOMPUTERS

PERHAPS YOU have already begun to explore uses of microcomputers and other electronic equipment for time and expense record-keeping, for instance. If so, then you will easily see how electronic office equipment of varying complexity can be applied to promoting and selling your design services as well. Whether these devices seem to you to be "small budget" marketing techniques depends on your annual gross income and staff size. Jim Mitchell, who in 1983 headed the national AIA's Computers and Architecture Committee, says that any office with more than three people can benefit from a computer of some sort. The question for most of us is having the cash to make such an investment. Even that is not an insurmountable problem since most manufacturers will lease you quite an elaborate set-up for less than $200 a month—tax deductible of course.

SOFTWARE

BUYING OR acquiring a small computer is rather like shopping for stereo record and tape playing equipment: You need to figure out what you are going to do with it before you begin to pick out the shiny machines. Every computer expert says the same thing. Don't buy anything until you have carefully assessed your business needs and thought them through (perhaps by taking a course at a community college). The process after all is exactly the same as preparing a design program before sketching begins.

Software is the encoded tapes or disks that tell the machines—the hardware—what to do. For marketing, the software is generally standardized and easily available. You do not need to master programming or even understand computer language to use these materials. BASIC is the most common language used in personal and microcomputers, although English is making big strides. For more complex business, math or science applications, some small computers can accommodate the COBOL, FORTRAN, and PASCAL languages as well. Another set of mysterious acronyms are CP/M (trademark of Digital Research Inc.), DOS, and UNIX. These are names of various disk operating systems, the internal control mechanisms that activate the computer and enable you to find and work with information on whichever software program you have inserted in the machine.

Preprogrammed software—which for small computers is usually on a 5¼″ diameter plastic circle permanently housed in a paper sleeve and called a "floppy disk" or "diskette"—is sometimes characterized by the amount of information it can hold. One with 140 Kb capacity holds the approximate equivalent of seventy double-spaced 8½ × 11-inch typewritten sheets, for example. What matters more, when one is considering which microcomputer to acquire, is whether the disks it uses are single or double sided, single or double density, soft or hard sectored.

Systems which are compatible with the second characteristic in each case, that is, double-sided, double-density hard disks, may be more expensive to purchase but worth it for increased speed and storage capacity, say Andrew and Carole Kass, who are partners in a Manhattan-based computer consulting firm, The First Word Incorporated. Every computer has a certain amount of built-in memory as part of its activating program: 64 Kb RAM means that the machine's Random Access Memory has enough capacity to operate most types of software that a small design office would use.

HARDWARE

THERE ARE FOUR distinct types of equipment beyond the standard electric correcting typewriter that can be useful for marketing purposes:

ELECTRONIC TYPEWRITER. At least two major manufacturers offer a sophisticated typewriter that has up to 16 KB of memory as well as justifying capability (holding a constant margin on the right-hand side as well as on the left). Will Ching has one that is programed to write prospecting letters. These machines also offer proportionally spaced type to simulate the appearance of the printed page. The results are quietly elegant on the page for a cost of $1,500 to $2,000, about 50 percent more than a self-correcting office typewriter. (All figures cited in this discussion are as of 1983.)

WORD PROCESSOR. A computer with restricted capabilities, the word processor is also less expensive. If you determine that the software needs of your office are predominantly in the word processing category (as they will be for most marketing purposes) rather than data processing, you may want to begin with this system, as UDA Architects have. Price is probably the advantage of the word processor, although before you decide on that basis, be sure that you are buying a machine that can do the same things as a computer costing that amount. A basic word processor and printer configuration (without data processing) is under $5,000, and prices are dropping.

PERSONAL COMPUTER. Since this is the system with which many manufacturers are competing for the home and small business market, it is anyone's guess how prices will drop and capabilities increase in the next few years. Personal computers all offer word processing software programs as well as many other capabilities. If your office requires a substantial amount of data processing capacity (such as engineering calculations or financial analysis), then consider these small computers. The system consists (not unlike the word processor) of four elements:

1. *Microprocessor:* The "black box," as it is known, is the heart of the computer. In it is the operating program such as CP/M or DOS, which reads the floppy disks when inserted.

2. *Keyboard:* It enables the operator to type in commands and information; it is integral with the display screen on less expensive models or connected by a coaxial cable.

3. *VDT (visual display terminal):* The monitor provides visual display of the information in monochrome—usually green or blue on black— or color (home computers often use a standard television set as a monitor and may be used for basic business functions, but they are not recommended for design office use).

4. *Printer:* It delivers a paper record of the information on the computer screen. There are both dot-matrix and "daisy-wheel" or letter-quality (looks like typewriter characters) printers. Some print slowly

(and are less expensive); others print quite rapidly. The dot-matrix type also has graphic capabilities. Letter quality is important if you intend to generate personalized letters with your computer. Such printers cost about $1,500 to $2,000, although there are many less expensive models available; an accessory that feeds letterhead stationery to the printer can add another $1,800 to the cost. Another useful accessory, if you elect to send the information directly to a service bureau for printing or to a printer, is a "modem" telephone hook-up ($300). The cost of a personal computer without printer ranges from $1,500 to $6,000 depending upon memory capacity, software programs selected, and other accessories chosen. Research your choices carefully. Finally, an option that should not be ignored is the service contract, generally figured in as 1 percent of the purchase price per month with a surcharge for "fast response" (less than four hours).

MICROCOMPUTER. Although the personal computer is a form of microcomputer, there are many more sophisticated options offered on customized systems than the personal computer packages sold. It is directly analagous with packaged stereos versus component sound systems. Jordan/Mitchell's system is an assembly of components. Jaffe Acoustics recently acquired a hard-disk computer (the storage capacity of a "hard-disk"—Winchester—over floppy disks is about 10 times greater) that they use for acoustical engineering calculations as well as for accounting and word processing purposes from more than one workstation. The cost was about $7,000 without a printer. If you feel the need for a customized system, be prepared to sort through endless options that will be eagerly offered to you by a dozen companies. You are now definitely beyond the "small budget" category.

SPECIFIC MARKETING APPLICATIONS

THERE ARE a wide variety of ways that you can use a microcomputer in your marketing plan.

MAILING LISTS. The most important role in promoting your services that a computer can play is storing lists of prospects, former clients, and other people to whom you send periodic mailings. If you choose to do direct mailings more than once a year, then the time saved by the equipment may well pay for it in two or three years. By coding the entries in your master address list onto database software, you can call forth the appropriate names for a dozen different kinds of mailings and print the labels automatically. Most personal computers easily accommodate up to a thousand names and addresses. Remember, however, that someone must spend time compiling and maintaining these lists.

PERSONALIZED LETTERS. A widely marketed piece of software, "MailMerge" (trademark of MicroPro), offers you the ability to prepare an appropriate letter for one of your markets for which it will automatically merge specific names, addresses, and salutations from your mailing list. This is the function where a letter-quality printer that accepts your business stationery makes a difference. It allows you to send out many more focused letters than a marketing-support person could generate during business hours. It frees that individual to do more research or to make personal contact by telephone or travel. Follow-up is also much easier when the letter is largely put together by the computer.

PROPOSALS AND REPORTS. Mitchell says that with the assistance of

Photo: Courtesy IBM

A "personal computer" consists of a keyboard attached to the microprocessor by a flexible cable, video display terminal (VDT) atop the microprocessor, and a matrix printer unit.

Estimate of Hours Breakdown

Construction Value	$292,500	
Project Compensation (Fee)	$ 38,000	
Estimated Reimbursables	$ 1,500	
Estimated Total Revenue	$ 39,500	
Fee Percentage of Construction		12.99%
Revenue Percentage of Construction		13.50%
Hourly Billing Rate	$ 40.00	
Internal Breakeven Hourly Rate	$ 32.84	

	Trial		Value	
	%	$ Value	$	%
Project Revenue		38,000	38,000	100
Profit (−)	10		3,800	10
Contingency (−)	10		3,800	10
Balance for All Expenses			30,400	80
Outside Services				
Structural		2,500	2,500	7
Mechanical		3,500	3,500	9
Electrical		1,500	1,500	4
Cost		650	650	2
Hardware				
Lighting		500	500	1
Civil				
Landscape				
Interior				
Graphic				
Special				
Miscellaneous				
Subtotal of Outside Expenses			8,650	23
Balance for In-House Expenses			21,750	57
In-House Direct Expenses				
Miscellaneous	4		1,520	4
Subtotal In-House Direct			1,520	4
Balance for Architectural			20,230	53

ARCHITECTURAL HOURS ESTIMATE

In this portion the services are estimated either by percent of total hours or by the hours to be spent on them (*not* both simultaneously). Note that the rate used to calculate number of hours available is the internal breakeven rate rather than the billing rate.

1. Predesign Services
   Programing
   Other
   Administration
   Subtotal: Predesign

		Trial	Value		
	%	Hours	$	Hours	%
2. Site Evaluation					
General					
Administration					
Subtotal: Site Evaluation					
3. Schematic Design					
Design	75	2,463		75	12
Other	10	328		10	2
Administration	25	821		25	4
Subtotal: Schematic	110	3,612		110	18
4. Design Development					
Architectural Design	100	3,284		100	16
Other	25	821		25	4
Administration	35	1,149		35	6
Subtotal: Design Development	160	5,254		160	26
5. Working Drawings					
Architectural Design	95	3,120		95	15
Specifications	25	821		25	4
Other	15	493		15	2
Administration	40	1,314		40	6
Subtotal: Working Drawings	175	5,748		175	28
6. Bidding					
General	25	821		25	4
Administration	10	328		10	2
Subtotal: Bidding	35	1,149		35	6
7. Construction Administration					
Shop Drawings	30	985		30	5
Site Visits	50	1,642		50	8
Other	25	821		25	4
Administration	30	985		30	5
Subtotal: Construction Administration	135	4,433		135	22
8. Postconstruction					
General					
Administration					
Subtotal: Postconstruction					
9. Supplementary Services					
General					
Administration					
Subtotal: Supplementary					
Total			$20,196	615	100%
Amount over (−) or under Budget			$34		0%

Computer allows you to determine compensation for negotiating with a client, based on reliable cost figures derived from your own records.

his firm's computer, "We have, for instance, produced a thirty-page proposal in one day when required. Being able to incorporate major portions of previous proposals (edited on the VDT to meet the needs of the job at hand) greatly speeds the process and also reduces the possibility of typos." Marketing reports—which include analyses of time spent on it, leads uncovered, calls made, reports intended for clients, and so on—are easily displayed on the VDT. All this material can be printed immediately if needed.

TYPESETTING. Another computer application is in-house preparation of material for typesetting. Jordan-Mitchell uses it for such items as current project lists, biographies, and photocards for presentations, which can be inexpensively typeset by preparing the text using the word processor or word processing software. The floppy disk can be handed directly to the typesetter, eliminating the cost of keying it into their typesetting equipment and then proofreading it. By using access codes from the printer, you can specify many different typefaces and sizes for presentation board titles and for charts that can be incorporated into slideshows. It is much faster than either office typesetting machines like Kroy or hand-applied pressure-sensitive letters, although turnaround may take another day or so.

FINANCIAL PROJECTION AND ANALYSIS. This is what the computer does best. Every small computer manufacturer offers "spreadsheet" (simulated bookkeeping page) programs for accounting and other record-keeping. In addition to storing these data, a spreadsheet program enables you to speculate about how your marketing program will be affected as key variables are changed. Known as the "what-if" situation, this software makes the computer a remarkable planning tool. Your economic projections can be modified instantaneously to give, for instance, both the maximum and minimum staff needs over as long as the next three years based on the estimated new business you project.

ESTIMATING FEES. Of all the accounting functions related to marketing, none is more important than the ability to accurately estimate how much it will cost to do a particular project. Jordan/Mitchell keeps all its time records on the computer using the AIA phase and detail coding (see example on pages 154–155), although any accounting system can be used. Truly complete work records permit documentation of compensation proposals that the prospective client is not likely to argue with. In addition, the spreadsheet program allows rapid estimating of alternative fees or hours available for a given fee in detail that is otherwise impossible. J/M's calculations of time available for a job, by the way, begin by taking 24 percent off the total budget for profit, contingencies, and direct expense and then dividing the rest by applicable hourly rates.

SCHEDULING. Software programs that allow you to create bar chart schedules and other graphic presentations on the personal computer do not require any of the plotting hardware associated with computer-aided design and drafting (CADD). The images can be reproduced by a standard printer. The advantage of doing such charts on the computer is that several schedules, each with different time or budget constraints, can be prepared in the time that one hand-drawn chart would take.

SELLING POTENTIAL. An intangible advantage of the computer that Mitchell points out is this: Such speed and accuracy in preparing information related to the time and cost factors of a job will no doubt influence a potential client to hire your firm. The time will come when computers no longer amaze people. For the present, however, it is possible that a small design office with a computer may win a commission or two because of its computer's businesslike image.

Computer Information Sources

General. Computer experts urge those contemplating the purchase or lease of equipment to familiarize themselves with the field and its potential by taking an introductory course. The important thing, they say, is that you must determine your specific computer requirements before selecting hardware.

Books
Computer-Aided Architectural Design by William J. Mitchell, New York: Van Nostrand Reinhold, 1977.
Computer Applications in Architecture and Engineering, G. Neil Harper, ed., New York: McGraw-Hill, 1968.
Computers in Architectural Practice by Natalie Langue, New York: Van Nostrand Reinhold, 1983.
Reflections on Computer Aids to Design and Architecture, Nicholas Negroponte, ed., New York: Petrocelli/Charter, 1975.

Technical Information
Directory of Software and Systems for Design Professionals ($95) and *Directory of Design Firm Computer Users* ($40) both available from Design Compudata, 126 Harvard Street, Brookline, MA 02146.
How to Use Desktop Computers in the Professional Design Firm ($245) includes four 60-minute audiotapes, a demonstrator computer disk.
Microcomputer Hardware/Software Guide, MRH Associates, Box 11316, Newington, CT 06111.

Magazines. *Architectural Record* offers "The Computer" (July 1983). *Personal Computer* and *Personal Computer World* available on newsstand.

B. Checklist for Go/No-Go Decisions

A. Adherence to Marketing Plan
☐ Does the project meet our *design objectives/ goals*?
☐ Does the project fit our *target markets* as defined in our marketing plan?
☐ Does the project match our *target services*?
☐ Is the project within our *geographic reach*?
☐ Is the project consistent with our *minimum/ maximum project size* objectives?
☐ Does the project present us with an unusual opportunity to break into a *new market* that we hadn't foreseen?
☐ Does the project offer *repeat client* potentials?
☐ If we get this job, will it *preclude* us from further work with this client?

B. Profit Potential
☐ Can we make a *profit* doing this job? (You might assign a range of points by profit potential.)
☐ Are there any *prevailing reasons* to want the job even though we can't make money on it?

C. Project Solidity
☐ Are project *funds* secured? If not, how likely is it that they will be?
☐ Is the *client* experienced or inexperienced in contracting design services?
☐ Is there a *discrepancy* between the proposed *scope* and the *fee*? Is the fee adequate? Can we propose a competitive fee?
☐ Are there *other factors* that negatively affect the project's viability?

D. Selection Process
☐ Is the *selection process* reasonable?
☐ Is the job *wired* to another firm?
☐ Can we *compete effectively* under the conditions of the selection process?

E. Odds
1. Skills and experience
☐ Do we have the *capability* to perform the work?
☐ Do we have a solid *track record/relevant experience* in the project type?
☐ Is the project the *right size* for us in terms of our objectives; our ability to compete; our ability to produce the work?
☐ If these are weak, do we have a *strategy or other credentials* to counterbalance these advantages?
☐ Will a *joint venture or association* be required to compete effectively? If so, are we prepared to form it? Will another firm put it together and do most of the marketing?

2. Location
☐ Is our *location* favorable in terms of the client's criteria?

3. Manpower
☐ Do we have the *available manpower* to produce the work in the client's time frame?

4. Marketing staff
☐ Do we have the *staff and time* available to market this project in a first-class fashion?

5. Client contact
☐ Are we *known* by the client? Is it a past client with whom we have a good reputation? Have we become known by the prospect?
☐ Will we have adequate opportunity to *research* the client's needs before the selling process begins?
☐ Do we have any *inside tracks* with the primary decision-maker? With others who are or may be influential in the decision?

6. Competition
☐ Who is the likely *competion*? Do we have a chance against them?
☐ Does this project offer us an opportunity to compete at a "*higher level*" against firms with whom we would like to be identified in the marketplace?

7. Message
☐ Do we have a strong "*message*"? What do we have that makes us uniquely qualified to do the job? To compete effectively?

8. Odds calculation
The odds are calculated on the basis of the answers to the questions above. They should be recalculated at each step in the selection process.
☐ What are our odds of *being shortlisted*?
☐ What are our odds if/when we *make the shortlist*?

If your odds are 50 percent that you will be shortlisted and 25 percent that you will be selected, then your odds are .50 × .25, or 12.5 percent. You might consider assigning a range of points based on your odds or determining a minimum odds percentage for pursuing an opportunity.

F. Cost to Pursue
☐ How much *marketing time and effort* will be required in proportion to our *odds*?
☐ What are the *marketing costs* relative to the potential *profit*? (Spending your profit to get the job may be sufficient reason to decide no-go.)

Developed by Carol McConochie. Published by A/E Marketing Journal, January 1981.

SELECTED BIBLIOGRAPHY

The A/E Marketing Handbook: A User's Manual, by Sandy D'Elia, Jim Ricereto, and Margaret Spaulding. Newington, Conn.: A/E Marketing Journal, 1983. Includes examples, press releases, call reports, SF 255s.

Architectural and Engineering Salesmanship, by David Cooper. New York: John Wiley, 1978.

The Art of Plain Talk, by Rudolph Flesch. New York: Collier (Macmillan), 1951 (8th printing, 1974). Anyone can learn to speak and write more clearly just by reading this or any other of Flesch's books and working through the exercises provided.

Bacon's Publicity Checker. Chicago: Bacon's Publishing Co. Loose-leaf guide to periodicals, updated annually. Includes names of editors, scope of publication, deadlines.

Creative Communications for a Successful Design Practice, by Stephen A. Kliment. New York: Whitney Library of Design, 1977. A thorough compilation of writing and other presentation skills that focuses on the specific needs of architects and other designers; includes copious illustrations and examples.

Design Presentation: Techniques for Marketing and Project Presentation, by Ernest Burden. New York: McGraw-Hill, 1983. Covers topics from planning presentations through the arcane technicalities of creating professional displays.

"Direct Mail Marketing," by Stephen A. Kliment. Reprint from March 1979 *Professional Services Management Journal*, Box 11316, Newington, CT 06111. What you can and cannot expect direct mail to do for you. Information on lists and costs.

Financial Management for the Design Professional, by Lowell V. Getz and Frank Stasiowski. New York: Whitney Library of Design, 1984. Contains special chapters on contract negotiation and pricing your services for profit.

A Guide to Business Principles and Practices for Interior Designers, by Harry Siegel, with Alan M. Siegel. Rev. ed. New York: Whitney Library of Design, 1982. A valuable sourcebook for efficient and profitable operation of interior design practices that applies to most other design disciplines as well.

The Home Video Book, by Bruce Apar and Henry Cohen. New York: Amphoto, 1982. Practical tips on creating your own video programs.

How to Market Professional Design Services, by Gerre Jones. 2nd ed. New York: McGraw-Hill, 1983. This is a sophisticated analysis of business development aimed at designers and others who are essentially professional marketers and large firm oriented.

How to Prepare Professional Design Brochures, by Gerre Jones. New York: McGraw-Hill, 1976.

Interior Design for Profit, by Mary Knackstedt. New York: Kobro Publications, 1980. An introduction to practice, this book also offers a discussion of the role that marketing plays in developing a sound design services business.

Managing Architectural and Engineering Practice, by Weld Coxe. New York: John Wiley, 1980.

Marketing Architectural and Engineering Services, by Weld Coxe. 2nd ed. New York: Van Nostrand Reinhold, 1982. This is the book that first showed architects and designers the path to success by developing new and interesting business.

Marketing and Promotion for Design Professionals, by John P. Bachner and Naresh K. Khosla. New York: Van Nostrand Reinhold, 1977.

Preparing Design Office Brochures: A Handbook, by David Travers. 2nd ed. Santa Monica, Calif.: Arts & Architecture Press, 1983.

"Preparing Effective Proposals." Reprint from *Professional Services Management Journal*, Box 11316, Newington, CT 06111. Covers strategy, costing, handling the SF 254 and 255 forms.

Pricing and Ethical Guidelines: Graphic Artists Guild Handbook. 4th ed. New York: Graphic Artists Guild Inc., 1982. A broad range of professional practices for illustrators, designers, and other graphic artists are covered; includes a number of standard contract forms.

Promoting Professional Services, by Stuart Rose and Vilma Barr. Washington, D.C.: Professional Development Resources Inc., 1978.

Public Relations for the Design Professional, by Gerre Jones. New York: McGraw-Hill, 1980.

Publicity Made Easy, by Robert Heming. Rockville, Md.: Publicity and Media Resources, 1979. Designed as a general introduction to publicity opportunities, this book includes a set of worksheets to help in preparing press releases and other public relations materials.

Selling Your Graphic Design and Illustration, by Tad Crawford and Arie Kopelman. New York: St. Martin's Press, 1981. An up-to-date marketing, business, and legal guide aimed primarily at graphic designers and illustrators with pricing information on a variety of assignments.

Videocassettes: *How to Use Video in Marketing*, 1983 and *Successful Presentation Strategies*, 1983. Both from PSMJ-TV, 126 Harvard St., Brookline, MA 02146.

Visual Presentation: A Practical Manual for Architects and Engineers, by Ernest Burden. New York: McGraw-Hill, 1977.

INDEX

Edited by Stephen A. Kliment and Susan Davis
Designed by Bob Fillie
Graphic production by Hector Campbell
Set in 11 point Clearface